The Gorbachev
Phenomenon

The Gorbachev Phenomenon

A History of Perestroika

Françoise Thom

Translated by
Jenny Marshall

Pinter Publishers, London and New York
in association with John Spiers

© Françoise Thom, 1989

First published in Great Britain in 1989 by
Pinter Publishers Limited
in association with John Spiers
25 Floral Street, London WC2E 9DS

British Library Cataloguing in Publication Data
A CIP catalogue record for this book is available from the British Library

ISBN 0–86187–

Printed and bound in Great Britain by
Short Run Press Ltd.

Library of Congress Cataloging-in-Publication Data
Applied for

Contents

Introduction

Since Mikhail Gorbachev came to power in March 1985 the eyes of the world have been fixed on the hotheaded General Secretary, focus of so many conflicting expectations. Some hope that he will at last realise the promise of socialism.[1] Others, like Margaret Thatcher, wonder whether he is not a closet ultra-liberal trying to lead the USSR away from socialism; still others see him as a disciple of Swedish-style social democracy. The American author Joyce Carol Oates admires his 'disarming candor', and has 'the gut conviction that Gorbachev is a person of matchless integrity, larger than life, perhaps'. A militant pacifist compares him to Jesus: 'He is always offering us goodly things, like disarmament proposals. . . . ' Anyone not sharing the faith in this new Messiah is immediately suspect: 'We may be wrong [about Gorbachev], but I prefer that error to the other, monstrous one, of doubt', says Pierre Bergé.[2]

This enthusiasm, reminiscent of past ages, is contrasted by the reservations expressed by many Soviets about their leader and the wariness and disenchantment evident in a number of independent publications, especially since the autumn of 1988. The greatest danger in 'Gorbymania' is that it leads us to forget that Gorbachev is not a legitimately-elected head of state, and therefore not representative, and that the USSR is more than the CPSU General Secretary, even when he is promoted to President.

This study aims to give an inside view of Gorbachevism and to offer an interpretation of the events and reforms taking place in the Soviet Union. It is based on regular reading of the official Soviet press – and the independent publications – since 1985.

It is a rash thing to try to analyse a situation of unknown outcome, particularly one clouded by every kind of emotion, forecast and fantasy. 'New thinking' or otherwise, the USSR has not yet become a straightforward object for study. Writing about the current situation there is a risky business, not only because of the fluctuations of Soviet policy since the introduction of the famous slogan *perestroika* (generally translated as 'restructuring'), but more importantly because this country, little known to foreigners, has until recently been buried in self-ignorance and is only now, clumsily and cautiously, starting to examine itself. *Glasnost* (best translated as 'publicity', in the sense of publicising a discussion)[3] is now instructing Soviet citizens and the rest of us that the USSR under Stalin displayed to the world an elaborate stage-set of thriving building projects and idyllic collective farms, all concealing a bloody and tragic reality of innumerable mass graves, peasants reduced to serfdom in the twentieth century, and a terrorised proletariat deprived of the most fundamental rights. Later, under Brezhnev, a carefully-laid carpet of false statistics demonstrated huge harvests and 'accelerated rhythms', under which mouldered corruption, cynicism and total economic breakdown.

And now? Has *glasnost* painted a complete picture of the USSR, or is the new-found volubility of the official press simply hiding 'no-go areas' more effectively than the surreal propaganda of Brezhnev's time? Experience should teach caution. In writing this study, I have taken care to erect barriers around some of the pitfalls in the area.

First, I have concentrated on social and political reality in the Soviet Union. *Perestroika* is incomprehensible without understanding of the problems it aims to combat. To describe the mess which the current Soviet regime has inherited has been my first task. My approach has been historical, even though *perestroika* is scarcely four years old, examining the events, decrees and decisions of the new regime, and analysing their causes and consequences.

I have carefully avoided being caught up in 'Kremlinology', from conviction that no information about the workings of the Politburo, personal conflicts, or the game of 'conservatives' vs. 'reformers' can be considered reliable or even perhaps important.

This is therefore not an examination of Gorbachev the man. Since 1917, there have been three moving forces in the Soviet Union: the Communist Party, ideology and the society itself. Taking place in the USSR today is a mortal struggle between a ruling power which feels threatened but will make no essential concessions and a society barricaded behind passive resistance. This study aims simply to describe the features of the underground combat, the result of which we have yet to see.

NOTES

1. 'This is what I have been waiting 20 years for', exlaimed French Sovietologist Lilly Marcou on Gorbachev's nomination, adding: 'Mikhail Gorbachev has not disappointed me; on the contrary, he never ceases to amaze me by the magnitude of his reforms and the depth of his thought.' Lilly Marcou, *Les défis de Gorbatchev*, Paris: Plon 1988.
2. Quoted in *Commentaire*, no.40, Winter 1987–8, p.776
3. *Glasnost* was one of the dissidents' demands. In 1969 Solzhenitsyn wrote: 'Complete and frank *glasnost* is the first condition for a healthy society, our own included.'

1. The causes of Gorbachev's revolution

THE WESTERN REVIVAL

In the last decade or so the Kremlin has suffered a series of jolts, the first of which was the unexpected evolution of the 'correlation of forces' in the international arena. During the 1970s the situation had looked promising. The United States had lost the Vietnam War and appeared lastingly traumatised by the defeat. The oil crisis seemed bound to bring the West to its knees, destroying the capitalist system once and for all. Yet the United States soon regained a political willpower that found symbolic expression in the liberation of Grenada (an event which had immense impact on the Soviets, as it demonstrated that socialism* can be driven out). The capitalist nations not only took the oil crisis in their stride, but made a technological leap which widened the gap between themselves and the Communist-dominated states. More worrying still in Moscow's eyes, several Third World countries pulled themselves out of underdevelopment and joined the ranks of the bourgeois world. In short, as *Pravda* commented in 1986, 'the general crisis in capitalism does not imply the linear disintegration of the system: capitalism has not yet exhausted the resources of its development'.[1]

Internal stagnation was tolerable as long as international circumstances seemed to herald the collapse of capitalism and a new phase of world Soviet expansion. Conversely, Western revival compelled the Kremlin's leaders to look uneasily into the 'negative phenomena' which dog socialism in maturity and which, by the leaders' own admission, eventually endanger the foundations of Communist power. Gorbachevism is first and foremost a response to Reaganism. As *Pravda* says, quoting the *Statesman* of India, 'Gorbachev's initiatives aim to reverse the flow of tendencies and processes apparent in the wake of eight years of Reaganism'.[2]

THE CRISIS

The human factor
Seventy years of lies, terror, slave labour, purges, sudden about-faces and the destruction of the first-rate, have given birth in the USSR to a peculiar human breed which unhappily bears no relation to the ideal man forecast by Communist doctrine. The new man of the Communist scheme was to be an

---

*'Socialism' is used throughout in the way in which Soviet ideologists understand it: as the first stage in the building of 'Communism'.

ardent worker fuelled by revolutionary enthusiasm, a disciplined creature of simple needs, fanatically devoted to the Party. In fact, the Communist mill has generally produced quite a different article. The USSR seems increasingly subject to a 'boomerang effect'. In many areas, policies carried out with, in Communist terms, every appearance of success – and on which the totalitarian system is based – have slowly turned against the regime and now threaten its very existence, simply because they have succeeded too well. Early realisation of the practical failures of pure communism in the economy produced, in 1920, Lenin's New Economic Policy (admittedly intended to be temporary). In the social and ethical sphere, nothing like this happened. Stalinist represssion of some of the most glaring effects of the social 'permissiveness' of the 1920s and his cynical appeals to 'traditional values' prevented any similar stock-taking. But the problems generated at that time – destruction of the family, of human relationships by terror, hostility between generations, debasement of relations between the sexes – continued, and in sovspeak, 'deepened'. All these problems have been compounded by the Party's social policies based on what is now officially entitled 'the residuary principle', by which social funding was relegated to the back burner in the face of more pressing economic and political concerns. Regular reading of the Soviet press shows that the population is now calling the regime to account with increasing insistence and that it is becoming impossible to avoid the problem. Soviet media attention is not taken up only with morals, either: numerous articles have been written about public health and even public attitudes and opinions. Western misunderstanding of *perestroika* arises largely from underestimating the crisis in the 'human factor' in the Communist world. The picture is so black that it is best to let it be painted by the Soviet press itself, which can hardly be accused of exaggeration.

Public attitudes

Constant shortages and the Party's involvement in every aspect of life have indeed brought about a state of mind among Soviet citizens which has finally begun to alarm the authorities, as they see the dangers it creates outweighing the long-term advantages for the totalitarian system.

The hardship in which most Soviet citizens have lived ever since the revolution has bred a fierce misanthropy into which the satirical novelist Alexander Zinoviev gives some insight. 'We are enemies every one against the other, there is nothing between us but hostility,' remarks the author Zalyguine.[3] 'We are witnessing a strange process for which I can find no other world than "de-socialising"[4]. . .. With regard to the relationships of daily life, we are in the stone age.'[5] Everyone is a potential rival in the acquisition of goods and privileges. Each person dreams of taking out on others the daily humiliations to which he is subjected in the endless queues, on the overcrowded trams and buses, at the workplace. 'We have no rights even in the simplest matters of daily life. Our dealings with hotel managers, railway officials, shopkeepers . . . are nothing but a series of humiliations . . . this lack of rights has an unlooked-for consequence – the desire to humiliate others in turn.'[6] Rudeness and aggression have become the rule. Denunciation runs wild – envy is poisoning all human relationships. 'One of our chief errors has been that while we were busy building a new world, we failed to notice the destructive force of envy . . . as long as we do not put a lid on envy, the success of *perestroika* is doubtful.'[7] *Pravda* prudently neglects to mention here that envy is the mainspring of socialism and that the passion for egalitarianism, now deplored by the authorities, has been drummed into the Soviet population for decades.

The absence of liberty, the habit of being under state care from childhood, and the systematic penalisation of personal initiative explain other character traits of the citizen under communism which the Party is beginning to perceive as dangerous. Chief among these is a firmly-rooted indifference: 'Indifference has become natural to us these past years. Those who suffer deeply are often seen as somehow abnormal.'[8] Indifference is the cause of many accidents. Refusal to assume responsibility is considered no less worrying – as in the case of the ships's captain who, not daring to send an SOS signal without his superior's approval, let his own crew drown rather than take the decision himself.[9]

This passivity goes hand in hand with what the authoritities call 'parasite mentality': the tendency to expect the state to solve every problem of existence, a condition of dependence pushed to the extreme. Here again the 'new man' has learnt his lesson too well, to the detriment of the regime. 'Begging has entered our veins.'[10] 'Gradually, imperceptibly, the whole country has grown used to living on the backs of others, to consuming without producing.'[11] 'The system of administrative command* has left us the legacy of an intolerable phenomenon: parasitism.'[12] 'The parasite mentality is widespread: everyone believes that the state is rich and will provide everything necessary. Life requires that we resolutely rid ourselves of this mentality.'[13]

Morals and the family
Soviet literature and the press are continually lamenting the decline in morals. The factors mentioned above have led many people to the 'de-socialising' which is a characteristic of life under communism. Added to this is the eternal housing shortage: in 1988, there were 4 million young families waiting for a flat;[14] 15 per cent of the population has no individual accommodation; more than 100 million Soviet citizens have less than nine square metres personal living space.[15] Seventeen per cent of families (about 50 million people) live in communal apartments shared with other families

---

*Sovspeak term meaning the system inherited from Stalin now considered as having been untouched by Khrushchev's de-Stalinisation.

in dormitories.[16] It is easy to imagine the consequences of such over-crowding and lack of privacy.

The neglect of a demographic policy by the old regime is severely criticised in the press: 'Ignorance of the complexities of demographics has led us into carelessness and the lack of control over numerous aspects of demographic development', says *Pravda*;[17] the same article emphasises that a demographic policy should not have the sole aim of the 'raising the birthrate when it is low, but of improving the qualitative characteristics of the population'. The press mentions the increase in divorce: 347 per 1,000 marriages in 1986[18] – between 930,000 and 950,000 a year.[19] Women request 68 per cent of divorces. In 1970 there were 7.8 million one-parent families.[20] Each year 500,000 illegitimate children are born – about 9.8 per cent of total births (the figure is 21 per cent in the United States). According to *Isvestia* 'most divorce is the result of psychological incompatibility of the spouses'. There are recommendations to increase the number of marriage guidance counsellors[21] and especially to avoid interference by the collective, which only aggravates matters. Quite clearly, those who formerly rejected the concept of private life are now singing a different tune.

Another complaint appearing frequently in the press indicates more than anything else the breakdown of social bonds in the Soviet Union: the abandonment of infants at birth. *Pravda* reveals that 90 per cent of children in orphanages were abandoned by the mother at birth.[22] The number of these children is now increasing year by year and has now reached nearly a million, three times the figure in 1946.[23] According to newspaper reports, the cause of these abandonments is general indifference, lack of group pressure, loss of the maternal instinct: 'If a contemporary artist were to undertake a portrait of the modern Madonna and child, he would be hard put to find a model. . . .'[24] This touches on yet another 'boomerang effect': women's liberation, which has already become a pejorative term in the USSR.[25] Women have become coarse, drinking and cursing like men.[26] Many share the viewpoint ingenuously expressed in *Literaturnaya Gazeta*:

We find in the press an increasing number of articles devoted to the 'feminisation' of men and the 'virilisation' of women. . . . Many people are concerned that the matriarchate is not far off. . . . It is instructive to examine the female character in the mirror of our current literature. . . . What are the constant factors? . . . Alcohol . . . no other way to get a man. . . . The total absence of love and above all, the recurring theme of our literature: women taking the initiative. And as for men? Either, like Joseph in the Bible, they resist forbidden caresses (sometimes perfectly legitimate conjugal ones) or they tear themselves free of feminine wiles; or they just let themselves go. Masculine initiative has become the prerogative of negative characters, while the heroes and semi-heroes have only one idea – how to get a free drink and steal away before 'payment' is exacted.[27]

Pravda published a letter from a woman saying: 'In my opinion, the state should make it its business to increase the authority of men. They have become very weak.'[28] The criticism is mutual to all appearances. Men accuse women of being unfeminine, women complain about male wimpishness.

To judge by the press, the women's lot is still the harder. Not only does she bear the consequences of the virtual non-existence of contraception (only 10 to 15 per cent of Soviet citizens use contraceptives; there are 11 million legal abortions every years in the USSR – a quarter of the world's total – in addition to the considerable number of illegal abortions which cause the death of 600 women a year in the RSFSR (Russian Federated Socialist Republic) alone[29]). But she also works in often dreadful conditions – nearly 3.5 million women are employed in conditions below acceptable safety standards and 4 million work at night.[30] Women have the exhausting job of queuing, often returning home to a drunken husband and peevish mother-in-law. 'Of course we want to be beautiful, but that is an impossible dream' writes a *Pravda* reader.[31] Another adds: 'I could hardly be called a woman, though no one could call me a man either. . . . I tremble for my daughter. Will she also have to face the jostling in the stores, obscenities in the streets, brutality in hospital, not to mention the "abortariums". . . . It is hard to be a beast of burden at work and at home.'[32] As *Sovietskaya Rossiya* remarks, 'the poor woman, who thinks "equal rights" have done her a favour, has been reduced to slavery at home and at work, with only the occasional dreadful suspicion that her life is simply a term of penal servitude.'[33]

It is not surprising that a woman thinks twice before having a second child: while 80 per cent of young couples have a child in the first year of marriage, only one family in every four or five will have a second. In the RSFSR, 97 per cent of families are two- or three-person.[34] *Pravda* gives an account of the reaction of a paediatrician on hearing that a patient was expecting a third child: 'A third child? How dreadful! Whatever possessed you?'.[35] This has a bad effect on education, as mothers cosset their one child, who becomes a spoilt, weak creature lacking all willpower. Mothers take no hand in discipline or education, throwing all responsibility on the school.

The theory that it is above all the state that is responsible for the education of children was a profound social mistake . . . and interestingly – as we often find – this aberrant idea, the object of a huge propaganda campaign, was quietly buried in the end. But even when the ideological bubble finally burst, many people retained an ironclad conviction that only the state and the schools were responsible for children's education.[36]

The effects of the fading-away of the father and maternal overprotection on the character formation of the Soviet youth, particularly his attitude to the law, would make an interesting psychological study.

SOCIAL PROBLEMS

'Decapitalisation' and poverty

The phenomenon of 'decapitalisation' – evident in all 'people's democracies' and the USSR as well – occurs when the state can no longer repair its buildings, roads, railroads and industrial equipment. In the USSR the roads are crumbling faster than they are being built.[37] In the summer pipes are left unrepaired so that in winter whole urban neighbourhoods are left without central heating for weeks; in some towns it is not unusual to have the hot water cut off for months at a time.[38] Official figures give some idea of the extent of the problem: nearly a third of towns in the RSFSR suffer from lack of water; there is insufficient heating in 42 industrial centres; only 7 per cent of rural dwellings are supplied with gas;[39] more than 300 towns have no water mains;[40] half the schools have no central heating or running water.[41] Roofs leak, bridges collapse, trains derail. The postal service is less and less efficient – in some regions mail is no longer even delivered. In Frunze all the letterboxes have been sealed.[42] The average speed of trains has been decreasing since 1976, and an express now travels at 50km an hour.

This decapitalisation does not only indicate lack of finance. It reveals, above all, the indifference of everybody to everything, and the carelessness and improvidence of a population accustomed to irresponsibility and civic passivity.

The impoverishment of the state is coupled with that of the population. About 100 million people – 40 per cent of families – have an income of less than 100 roubles per person per month, the poverty line being between 50 and 90 roubles per person per month.[43] And poverty in the USSR means a different thing from poverty in the West. Many goods cannot be obtained at all without backhanders; clothes are extremely expensive; and fruit and vegetables, often unavailable in state shops, cost a fortune at the collective farm markets where surplus produce may be sold. An average Soviet family spends 59 per cent of its income on staple foodstuffs.[44] Of course, theft from the state, practically universal in the USSR and hardly even condemned, permits some improvement of lifestyle and helps to alleviate the constant hardship. It remains true, though, that at least a third of the Soviet population is to all intents and purposes pauperised. Furthermore, official figures[45] put the number of vagrants at 1 per cent of the population, and 2 per cent of adults are unemployed – certainly well below the true figure.

Ecological problems

The list of ecological disasters presented by the media is ever-lengthening. Tashkent is threatened by drought, as are Armenia,[46] Leningrad[47] and Odessa.[48] The whole Leningrad region is turning into a foetid swamp.[49] Lake Ladoga is polluted with phosphorous, the Aral Sea has lost 66 per cent of its volume and may disappear altogether. The evaporation has already created a desert of some 25,000 square km around the shore, and the water level is falling by 90 cm a year.[50] The Azov Sea is polluted. The Volga basin, all the region around Kursk, the Syrdaria and Amoudaria Rivers, Kalmoukia and the industrial areas of the Urals, have all been declared ecological disaster areas.[51]

In 104 Soviet towns pollution exceeds acceptable levels more than ten times, and a quarter of tap water is contaminated.[52] Pollution is increasing rapidly, to judge by Moscow, where there has been a 6 per cent increase in the last two years.[53] Numbers of articles have linked the rise in infant mortality to pollution levels and the abuse of chemical fertilisers and pesticides. In May 1987, at the Plenum of the Writers' Union, one of the participants remarked: 'Our descendants will be born and die today.'[54] A delegate at the 19th CPSU Conference declared: 'If today we do not fight energetically to preserve the well-being of the environment as we fight against chemical and nuclear weapons, against war in general, we risk smothering ourselves before any war breaks out.'

Health
'We are all ill nowadays', said *Literaturnaya Gazeta* on 11 November 1987. The official Soviet media are no longer bothering to conceal the general bad health of the population. Newspapers are instead reproaching citizens for letting themselves fall sick, seeing it as a sly way of avoiding civic obligations. 'The health of citizens belongs to the people. A Soviet citizen is obliged to be in good health.'[55] The reason for the authorities' new interest in the health of the population is obvious: 'Health is an indispensable condition to increasing productivity.'[56] Various details handed out sparingly by the media since *glasnost* in 1985 establish some record of Soviet health.

According to Public Health Minister Yevgeny Chazov, the USSR comes 32nd in the world for life expectancy,[57] at 65 years for men and 67 for women (in the USA it is 73 and 77 respectively).[58] During the period of 'stagnation', (the Brezhnev era) life expectancy dropped at a dizzying rate.[59] In 1987 72 million people were hospitalised.[60] In 1986–7, 4 million people a day took sick leave (700,000 of these to care for a family member).[61] In 1986 30 per cent of pregnant women were found on medical examination to have other diseases unrelated to their pregnancy.[62] The number of premature births is increasing, which partly accounts for the increase in infant mortality. In an interview for *Sovietskaya Rossiya*, a paediatrician, Dr Tabolin, declared that 18 out of 1,000 newborns died shortly after birth (in 1987 in France it was 7.6 out of 1,000). Out of every 1,000 Soviet infants 30 do not live beyond the first year.

But these numbers must be taken with a large pinch of salt: a surprise count of Uzbekistan revealed that the real figure for infant mortality was 4 times higher than that indicated by statistics from hospitals, which naturally take care not to produce figures which are too disastrous. Dr Tabolin says that Soviet medical statistics are often rigged to correspond better to those of Western countries. It would otherwise be puzzling that the Soviet medical establishment should worry so much about the number of premature births and stillbirths, when the official figures compare fairly well with those in Western democracies. It is known that some newborns are not registered until such time as they seem likely to survive.[63] According to official figures, in

1987 12,000 stillborn babies were registered in the USSR[64] (5,615 in France). Infant mortality among premature births (4.5 per cent of premature births, compared to 5 per cent in France) is over 20 per cent.[65] Of all children born 5 per cent have serious genetic deformities;[66] 2.5 million suffer from spasticity as a result of birth trauma[67] and 8 per cent of children born in Moscow are oligophrenic (mentally retarded).[68] The number of children suffering from diabetes, hypertension and hormonal imbalances is increasing alarmingly.[69] More than 53 per cent of Soviet schoolchildren have health problems (poor eyesight, digestive disorders and neurological troubles).[70] It is reported that 80 per cent of childhood ailments are caused by contaminated water.[71]

Adults are no better off. Fatalities from cardiovascular disease are nearly twice those in the developed countries.[72] Since the mid 1970s there has been an upsurge among adults of various childhood illnesses (measles, scarlet fever, whooping cough), which often take very grave forms in adults.[73] Digestive disorders, hepatitis, and diphtheria are 'causing a lot of problems'; 1.5 million people suffer each year from digestive ailments.[74] From 1965 to 1985, lung cancer claimed one million, the number having doubled over one period of ten years.[75] Soviet health officials have recently declared that AIDS will become a major problem in the USSR.

Added to these are various regional diseases. According to a Georgian physician, hepatitis B 'has nearly assumed the dimensions of a national problem'.[76] In May 1988 a typhus epidemic swept through Georgia. Malaria is widespread and there have even been recorded cases of cholera.[77] In Moldavia 13 per cent of the population carry the hepatitis B virus – giving a national average of 3.8 per cent, around 10 million people.[78] Each year 33,000 children die in Uzbekistan, mostly from contaminated water. In Kazakhstan 60,000 cases of tuberculosis have been counted.[79] In Turkmenistan 12 per cent of young men are declared physically unfit for military service.[80] Only 40 per cent of conscripts from Kirghizia are judged physically sound by the army[81] – this in a country in which very few young men are exempt from military service. In Karakalpakia life expectancy is around 40 years. In some areas of Uzbekistan 'mortality among newborns is over 50 per cent. In the Alat region it is 53.4 per cent, in Guijduvan 72.8 per cent.'[82]

What is the reason for the physical decay of the population, shown in official figures certainly well below the true ones? Experience of the grim ordeal of any encounter with Soviet medicine casts some doubt on the cynical explanation offered by Health Minister Yevgeny Chazov that 'free medical care leads people to neglect their health',[83] echoing *Pravda*'s comment that people in the United States enjoy better health because medicine there is expensive.[84] Various related factors probably account for the decline in health standards in the USSR.

The alcohol problem illustrates the workings of the 'boomerang effect' perfectly. Until recently the sale of vodka was highly advantageous to the regime. In the absence of consumer goods, sales of alcohol circulated money, guaranteed massive revenue to the State and anaesthetised the population. But now the stage has been reached where the evils are outweighing the advantages. The regime is suffering enormous losses in man-hours because of alcoholism. Not only must alcoholics have medical care, but the State is being left to look after an increasing number of deformed children born to alcoholics. Compensation must be given to the victims of road and work accidents caused by the effects of alcohol. Last, but not least, production suffers considerably on account of workers' hangovers. All this led to the present regime's severe criticism of Brezhnev's policies: 'Previous policies were designed to encourage drunkenness among the people, to prevent them reflecting on their lives or worrying about politics.'[85] Over the 11th 5-year plan (1981–5), taxes on alcohol brought the state 169 billion roubles (compared to 67 billion over the 8th 5-year Plan).[86]

In the USSR drinking begins early in life. Commenting on teenage alcoholism, *Literaturnaya Gazeta* has written that 'This anomaly has almost become the norm'.[87] According to official figures, over 90 per cent of alcoholics began drinking before the age of 15, a third before the age of 10 and 90 per cent were hardened drinkers by the age of 19. In the Soviet Union there are 4.5 million alcoholics registered by the police or the health services.[88] This figure is probably a pale reflection of the true one. A *samizdat* article distributed just before the introduction of Gorbachev's anti-alcohol campaign suggested a figure of 40 million. Women make up 12 to 15 per cent of alcoholics.

The drug problem is being raised more and more often. To go by official statistics, in 1987 50,000 addicts were in clinics in the USSR.[90] That compares favourably to Western countries, but the increase in drug addiction is disturbing. Each year, 3,000 addicts and 120–130,000 drug-abusers are sent to detoxification centres.[91] Drugs are spreading through the schools.[92] In one year in Georgia alone drug trafficking brought in a profit of 36.5 million roubles.[93] A campaign against drug addiction was launched in August 1987 in Moscow; anti-drug legislation was introduced in Tadzhikstan in that same year.[94] Also in 1987, 26,000 people were sentenced for drug-dealing.[95]

Recent articles, particularly in the military press, show that the amount of smoking in the USSR is beginning to worry the authorities. There are 70 million smokers in the Soviet Union[96] and 17 per cent of young people begin smoking around the age of 8 or 9; by the time they reach secondary school, 80 per cent are smokers.[97] Over 430 billion cigarettes are sold each year.[98] From 1970 to 1986, tobacco consumption increased by 23 per cent.[99]

Another disquieting factor is the Soviet diet, too high in sugar and fat, which contributes to the high rate of cardiovascular disease. Furthermore, many basic foods are unfit for consumption: in the Ukraine, for instance, 'fresh' cream must always be boiled to prevent food poisoning. Now, under *perestroika*, sausage, when available, turns green in the light.[100] Lack of fresh fruit and vegetables causes serious deficiencies of between 20–60 per cent of essential vitamins.[101] Misuse of fertiliser and pesticides renders many products toxic. Cases of fatal nitrate poisoning among children were recently reported.

How is Soviet medicine coping with this disaster? Public health receives 4 per cent of the national budget.[102] A remark by *Pravda* sums up the general impression: 'Today, Soviet medicine is a soldier armed with a bow and arrow.'[103] Nearly 30 per cent of Soviet hospitals have no sewage disposal facilities, while 35 per cent have no hot water.[104] Surgeons are obliged to buy thread for sutures at sewing shops.[105] 'Many hospitals are hotbeds of infection where filth reigns . . . there are often no sheets, crockery or thermometers' and in some areas there is an eight-month waiting list for hospital entry.[106] Medical care is provided free in theory, but in fact backhanders are the norm, with doctors and nurses receiving extremely low salaries. The situation is not surprising, considering that the 4th Directorate of the Ministry of Health, charged solely with the medical treatment of aged high-ranking Party members, absorbs 50 per cent of the public health budget.[107]

The press is not forthcoming on the subject of mental illness, depression and suicide. A figure for suicide was revealed in June 1988 for the first time since 1926, and gave the total as 20 out of 100,000; a total of around 56,000 a year[108] (in France, it is 21 per 100,000). This places the USSR third in the world suicide tables. Five million people were registered in psychiatric clinics when Gorbachev came to power; he ordered 2 million of them discharged, doubtless to combat the manpower deficit and the number of people 'escaping' from official work (to have a certificate of mental illness exempts the holder from military service and also from having to belong to a work collective).[109] The number of schools for mentally-handicapped children is increasing each year. According to a *samizdat* article, half the schools in Moldavia are of this type.

Accidents
According to official estimates, in 1986 accidents caused the death of 109 people in each 100,000 compared to 169 in 1980 and 145 in 1985. The improvement is attributed to the anti-alcohol campaign.[110] Each year, road accidents account for 40,000 fatalities and 250,000 injured,[111] a very high figure considering the very small number of motorists in the USSR. Alcohol and the bad condition of the roads are mainly responsible for these accidents.
4   The media have begun to mention fires, a problem aggravated by the nationwide shortage of extinguishers. *Pravda* reported a fire at a bus depot in Voronezh which destroyed 87 vehicles on 9 December 1986. Everyone was shocked by the fire at the library of the Leningrad Academy of Sciences in February 1988 in which thousands of unique volumes were destroyed. The number of blazes caused by exploding television sets has doubled since 1980.[112] In November 1987 90 fires were caused this way in Moscow.[113]

The press remains silent on the actual number of work accidents, but the number of indirect references suggests that they are very common. Railway accidents seem also to have been multiplying of late, probably due to Gorbachev's staff cutbacks in the railway system. From October to

December 1987 there were 48 railway accidents, more than a third up on the same period the previous year.[114] A surprising figure is given for deaths by drowning: 25,000 each year. In the RSFSR alone, 350,000 people have drowned over the past 20 years. The number of people who drown is 6.67 per 100,000 (compared to 1.4 in West Germany). A third of these drownings are due to drunkenness. A quarter of the victims are under 16 and do not know how to swim.[115] Among males, the number of fatalities from shock and poisoning is the highest in Europe (12 per cent).[116]

Youth

A 'state *samizdat*' document[117] has summed up the debate about youth which was first raised at the January 1987 CPSU Plenum. 'One of the most serious problems,' it says, 'which we face today is the problem of youth. We have lost the 15–20 age group. And we must recapture them or there will be no one to carry *perestroika* through.'[118]

In August 1985 *Literaturnaya Gazeta* began a series devoted to the problems of young people. Many previous articles had given warning signals. The newspapers began by criticising the 'racism against youth' prevalent in Soviet society, leading even to murder in some cases, as when an adult killed a teenager whom he had previously insulted without reason, simply because the boy came to him to demand an explanation.[119] Several times the series mentioned the complaints of adults claiming to be terrorised by groups of teenagers, who in turn accused their elders of persecuting them without rhyme or reason, and their parents of turning them out into the street. Some of the adults' letters evinced an undisguised hatred of the young.

The apathy and bureaucratisation of the Komsomol is held up as the cause of a breakdown in ideology among the young, which is taking forms worrying to the authorities: in Turkmenistan, for example, as *Pravda* notes, evasion of military service is applauded.[120] The disintegration of the family and the reduction of the Komsomol to a pure formality (in other words, the disappearance of the state as a family substitute) have had a more serious consequence: young people are forming gangs regulated only by street law. In the provinces and suburbs of major cities this phenomenon, which first raised its head in the late 1940s and the early 1950s, seems to be becoming the rule. The era of *glasnost* has furnished startling statistics on this particular form of 'de-socialisation'. Here, for instance, is what goes on in Kazan:

Children can join a gang from the age of 7 or 8. If anyone wishes to quit a gang, he is forced to buy himself out for 250 roubles. Previously, membership of a gang ended when a young man left to do his military service, but this is no longer the case. On his return from the army, he now takes his former place in the gang and remains in it sometimes until the age of 35. Each gang controls a territory and all the schools on its turf. Gang wars are fought with knives and bicycle chains, or even with firearms, explosives and grenades. Those killed are given a sumptuous funeral paid for by the gang. If the police arrest a gang member, it is not unusual for his gang to storm the police station and 'liberate' him. Gangs are concluding treaties and dividing towns up between themselves.

This was the case in spring 1988, when Kazan gang leaders got together to proclaim a 'month of love' – the main theme of which was to be the rape of any young girl daring to venture out alone.[121] The total number of gangs in Kazan is around 150. As a last resort, a curfew was introduced.

What must be the state of affairs in the multi-ethnic towns such as Alma-Ata, with Russians, Kazakhs fighting each other ethnic Germans and Chechenes (Muslim Caucasians)?

The most notorious gang is the *Lyubery* from the Moscow suburb of Lyubersty. The *Lyubery* meet in cellars for intensive physical training with a view to making themselves 'hard'. There are around 500 of them and membership requirements are to have taken part in a gang fight and shown that 'you're bright, polite and bad'. Their motto is: 'Let's clean up the filth!'. This last category includes those who have fallen under the influence of 'Western mass culture' and so fail to respect the 'Soviet way of life', financial speculators and those with 'illegal income'. The *Lyubery* come into Moscow in groups of 50 or 60, prowling the streets until they come upon someone whose looks they dislike (perhaps someone wearing a Western badge or T-shirt, or who looks like an intellectual). The gang accosts its victim, politely points out his heinous offence, beats him up and removes all non-Soviet clothing. These trophies, sold later on the black market, enable the *Lyubery* to support themselves in high style, even more so as they make a practice of exacting tributes from young speculators. Punks, 'metallisty' (hard rock fans) and hippies suffer most from the *Lyubery*. The police either turn a blind eye or take minimal action.[122]

It would be interesting to know whether the Fascist complexion of the *Lyubery* is specific to itself or is a general characteristic of teenage gangs. It may be the results of the attempts by the authorities to gain some influence over the gangs, notably through young veterans of the war in Afghanistan – *Afghantsy* – who are organising 'military-patriotic education clubs' under the aegis of regional party organisations. Nevertheless, it seems that the attractions of the street overpower those of the 'schools of heroism'. At Kokand a group of youths attacked some *Afghantsy*, killing one of them. At Kazan the formation of a military-patriotic club 'Kaskad' has not altered the situation: a new gang has simply been added to the others and street fights are raging more than ever. Official statistics show that juvenile delinquency is increasing sharply. Each year 900,000 teenagers have a run-in with the police.[123] In Moscow juvenile delinquency rose by 20 per cent in 1987.[124] In 1988 the general level of criminality rose by 17.8 per cent compared to 1987. The number of crimes committed increased from 558 per 100,000 in 1987 to 657 per 100,000 in 1988.[125] In 1988 16,710 murders were committed throughout the USSR.[126] In 1989 this trend has even got worse. During the first half of the year, crime rose by 32.1 per cent in comparison with the same period in 1988 (*Pravada*, 12 July 1989). Faced with this increasing threat, the authorities are perceiving the 'informal associations' as a lesser evil. 'There are few informal groups, and their influence on the younger generation is less bad than might be thought. The "territorial" groups are infinitely more dangerous. . . .'[127]

The Elderly

The press nowadays often refers to the deplorable conditions suffered by the elderly. In May 1985 a decree was issued raising the monthly pension of retired collective farm workers from 28 to 40 roubles (the average monthly salary is about 180 roubles). Over a third of pensioners live on less than 60 roubles a month, i.e. one third the income of the active population.[128] The average income of retired industrial and office workers is 83 roubles a month, and 53 roubles a month for retired collective farm workers.[129] Elderly people therefore continue to work as long as they have strength to do so. As for old people's homes, the papers are full of Dantesque descriptions: residents are robbed and neglected by the staff and terrorised by aged thugs. Homes are sometimes not even supplied with running water.[130]

The picture painted above may seem improbably hellish to a Western reader, but it is taken directly from Soviet official and academic sources. It is essential to understand the regime's perception of the 'human factor' in order to have a means of interpreting the basis of the Gorbachev phenomenon. Two passages sum up the insider's view particularly well. The first is from the famous Novosibirsk report on alcoholism, which appeared in the West at the end of December 1984:

No one is preparing to attack us. All the speeches about Pershing and strained international relations are just chatter. Who would start a war against us, when in 12–15 years we will have ceased to exist as a sovereign state . . . a state in which over half the population are alcoholics and drunkards is incapable of defending itself . . . in most Siberian villages everyone from the mayor to the cowherd drinks. Our institute grows all the beetroot for Akademgorodok because the entire village responsible for providing it is in a constant alcoholic stupor, so no one works. The most terrifying consequence of 20 years of alcoholic madness is the inexorable degeneration of the nation, especially the Russian areas. . . . What do we leave behind us today? This year – 1983 – we gave birth to so many handicapped babies that in 1990 at least 15 per cent of our children will be in special schools. . . . In Siberian villages people do not live beyond 60 because of drink. They go to work in the morning with only one idea – to get soused after lunch. In the evening you have as much chance of meeting a Martian as a sober person.[131]

In May 1987, the journalist A. Strelyany made a public declaration at a Komsomol conference in Moscow, of which a *samizdat* record has appeared in the West.

If we do not do something, if we do not make an enormous leap by the end of the 1990s, we will be left with a situation of ruin comparable with that at the end of the civil war . This winter has hit the towns hard, exposing everything – all the holes. A friend of mine, First Secretary of the Obkom [Oblast Party Committee – Oblast is the administrative level below Republic], is building houses in the countryside outside a city of more than a million inhabitants. Everyone asks him: 'Why bother?' He keeps quiet and smiles. To me, he says: 'Will it be for this winter? Or next?' That is the question that will not let him rest. If the town freezes, he will evacuate the population to the country.'[132]

More recently, Academician Leonid Abalkin has complained that the Soviet Union 'can buy machinery from the West, but not a new people. We will have realised in 20 years that our "ironclad victories" are simply the excrement of civilisation.'[133] *Sovietskaya Kultura* adds, quoting Pavlov: 'It is easy to turn man into a beast, but terribly difficult and unbelievably slow to make that beast a man again.'[134]

The population's moral and physical decay, paralleled by the obsolescence of industrial machinery, has finally begun to alarm the Soviet leaders because they see in the human and mechanical disintegration a direct threat to their power base. How can a modern army be run with ignorant, sickly and drunken soldiers? How can a computer revolution be achieved with a population that abhors all initiative? How can the Soviet people be put back to work and the engines of Communist power re-started for a new expansion? That is the main problem the Soviet leaders face, a problem as thorny as it is new to Soviet history. There is hardly any prescription in the traditional Leninist pharmacopoeia for a debilitated 'human factor'.

The people have ceased to believe, the people have ceased to work. Today it will be difficult to start the people moving so that they will work as unremittingly as after 1917. Our task is now to take such measures that the people will regain their confidence in us and will apply themselves to resolving the economic problems.[135]

The 'degeneration of the cadres'*
At the beginning of 1987 the authorities in the USSR steeled themselves to face the necessity of political reform. It is essential for Westerners to understand how Soviet leaders perceive the political problem in their country; otherwise we risk building our own conceptions on their analyses and thereby completely misunderstanding Gorbachev's political 'reforms'.

Their analyses boil down to this: Khrushchev's high-level de-Stalinisation was not coupled with a fundamental de-Stalinisation of Soviet society. Quite the contrary. As the Stalinist terror receded, the ruling cadres began to enjoy total liberty to act as they pleased; de-Stalinisation at high level resulted in a proliferation of small-scale Stalins ruling their patches in the good old tradition of fear and corruption. This structure has become entrenched throughout Soviet society: the collective farm president and economic enterprise director tyrannise their employees; the director of a research institute has discretionary powers over his subordinates (including the right to appropriate their discoveries); the Raikom (Rayon Party Committee – Rayon is the level below Oblast) secretary makes the rain fall or the sun shine in his area, but is in turn subject to the Obkom secretary, and so forth.

We talk a great deal about the consequences of Stalin's personality cult, without mentioning that later on our country as a whole, the republics and regions, were victims of similar evil. The objective cause of both large and small cults is absolutism. It is no secret to anyone that the power of, for instance, the First Secretary of a Regional or District Party Committee is unlimited. . . . He can ruin any functionary in 'his' territory and interfere in any business he cares to, including judicial business.[136]

As a letter to the editor of *Izvestia* points out: 'Too often our bureaucracy has been ungovernable from above and uncontrollable from below'.[137]

The most notorious case is that of Adylov, director of an agro-industrial complex in the Ferghana valley,[138] who was arrested in August 1984, but not before he had turned his area into a mini-state, complete with borders and a prison where the most refined tortures were practised. The locals were treated like serfs. Those brave enough to go to Moscow to complain were met on their return and disappeared into the underground prison. Adylov had a harem, a private restaurant, several dachas and a magnificent stable. He owned his immunity to Rachidov, First Secretary of the Uzbek Communist Party, who was protected in turn by Brezhnev and his clique. Those higher up could be induced to turn a blind eye by bribery and various other favours: banquets, rest cures, all sorts of services. As for the subordinates, they had no redress whatsoever against these abuses, even less so as regional judges and police were all bought up by the local satraps. Networks of absolute power were thereby created, escaping all control by central authorities and even managing little by little to corrupt them, with each official bribing his superior and a chain eventually being forged all the way to Moscow.

It may be asked why the central authorities were so worried about this state of affairs: after all, the totalitarian dream was to all intents realised. The population was firmly under the control of immediate dictators, and the system seemed stable, with no apparent threat of explosion. But various elements conspired to ruin the Brezhnevian idyll. In the first place, the central authorities began to realise that they were losing all control of the fringe; then came KGB and Army reports of the unpopularity and discredit into which the Party had fallen, reports which in the end found attentive ears; and the decline of the economy was becoming too glaring for any rigged statistics to disguise the empty shops. But something else eventually decided the introduction of *perestroika*. This was the threat posed to Party political purity by its relations with the Soviet 'mafia' network.

The Soviet media likes to elevate certain cases to the status of illustrative examples. The episode of Rachidov in Uzbekistan is now almost a required reference in any article about 'organised criminality', and the press revelled in the celebrated 'cotton scandal' for months after its disclosure. What really happened there? The resumé of a report compiled by the Prosecutor, V. I. Chistiakov – which had limited distribution in the Soviet Union and appeared in the West in the *émigré* journal *Strana y Mir*[139] – throws some light on the case, as do more recent press articles.

In 1959, Sharaf Rachidov was elected First Secretary of the Uzbek Party. To impress Brezhnev, he undertook to triple the cotton harvest. *Pravda* quoted an eyewitness:[140] 'Rachidov promised to deliver 5 million tonnes of cotton and more each year. I remember Leonid Illyich's answer as if it were today, "Make it 6 million, my little Sharaf!" and Rachidov replied, "as you wish, Leonid Illyich!".'

Thus was born in Uzbekistan a whole thriving bogus cotton industry which enabled local Party bosses to pocket handsome state bonuses, invest in non-existent plantations and pay wages to an imaginary labour force. Large bribes given to those firms 'in receipt' of the cotton encouraged them to ignore its absence, and the wave of corruption peaked in Moscow. In the end, the entire Ministry for the Cotton Industry was thrown in goal. The man in charge of this lucrative scheme was none other than the First Secretary of the Boukhara Obkom, who had accumulated 3.5 million roubles in bribes. Numerous Obkom and Raikom Secretaries, the President of the Uzbek Council of Ministers, the Deputy Minister of the Uzbek Supreme Soviet, and the Minister of the Interior of the USSR were all implicated in the affair. Altogether, 20,000 people were arrested in Uzbekistan.

But fraud in state enterprises is only a small part – and the least important one – of the evil. The development of criminal rackets (the Soviets themselves call them mafias) has depended largely on the growth of the parallel economy – the 'shadow economy', as the Soviet media call it. Throughout Brezhnev's time in power, private rackets developed within state enterprises, using raw materials belonging to the state as well as (nominally) state workers. The press held up the case of the 'Riabtsev firm' – a racket with an annual turnover of over 6 million roubles and with a finger in more than 60 state enterprises. It gave backhanders worth 400,000 roubles a year to various local Party officials to turn a blind eye to what was happening, and even to protect the network from state competition. When a member of the firm fell into the hands of the law, he would be able to call on high-level protection and be well provided for in prison. The enterprise had well-placed 'sponsors' and carried on its activities for over ten years. In the end, Riabtsev was shot.

This last case, reported by *Sovietskaya Rossiya*,[141] is extremely interesting as it shows the implications for the regime of the parallel economy and reveals what is behind the accusations of corruption levelled at cadres. The development of 'private enterprise' within state businesses was leading to unchecked privatisation of the whole industrial network. The state sector, little by little, was becoming an empty shell. What with theft, embezzlement and the creation of false jobs, it found itself furnishing the black economy with free labour and raw materials. 'Greater and greater sums from the state budget were passing into private hands.'[142] The state lost all along the line, as the wealth created by this parasitism escaped it entirely.

Then came the proliferation of the mafias. Crooked 'businessmen' were originally subject to extortion by gangsters who would 'shake them like plum trees'; but in the mid 1970s, a pact was concluded: the 'industrials' would pay a regular 'tax' (10 per cent of their profits) to the mafiosi in return for protection. The Uzbek mafia appeared around 1968, the Moscow one at the beginning of 1970. Under Stalin there had been individual thugs, but never mafias, as this phenomenon is 'impossible in a totalitarian state', as *Literaturnaya Gazeta* says. Over time, the Soviet mafia has become a massmovement; when a mafioso dies, he is given a sumptuous funeral which is really a show of strength against which the police are powerless. Such ceremonies have been held in Moscow, Tashkent, Rostov and Ashkabad.

This already grave situation was worsened by the fact that local Party functionaries were covering up the clandestine activity, as it brought them handsome profits (two-thirds of mafia income went to buy Party officials). Some even went so far as to undertake various money-making ventures themselves. 'Leading officials have become accessories to, and even orga- nisers of, criminal activity', noted Gorbachev in his address to the CPSU Central Committee Plenum in January 1987. In effect, the mafia was taking over the Party and state apparatus: 'During the Brezhnev era, mafiosi infiltrated right to the top of the hierarchy, exercising their influence not only on the economy but on the legislative process'.[143]

The mafia pyramid was not only growing but building itself inextricably into the pyramid of state power . . . the day the 'godfathers' were able to prise a section of the *nomenklatura* from levers of power, the gangsters would be able to assume complete control of our beloved bureaucracy.[144]

Most worrying of all in the eyes of the true Leninists is that the mafia is now not only a disciplined organisation, but to some extent enjoys the approval of the population. The godfathers have 'more than enough willing agents to do their work: ardent young extremists, *petit bourgeois* chafing at constant hardship, nationalist intellectuals and corrupt functionaries . . . sooner or later the godfathers will engage in the political battle, and most energeti- cally.'[145] In Uzbekistan 'the mafia is stopping at nothing, even going so far as to promote on the quiet the revival of Islam.'[146]

A humiliating detail for the Party is that its hierarchy is not respected by the mafia. With the exception of Rachidov and his sidekick Adylov, Party bigwigs occupy humble positions in mafia organisations. Readers of *Pravda* are left in no doubt that success in the mafia requires talents not possessed by bureaucrats. In an article on Brezhnev's corrupt son-in-law, Y. Churbanov (accused in January 1988 of having accepted the equivalent of 650,000 roubles in bribes), the paper says:

It is quite clear today that he was not a true boss. He was too mediocre for that. It is one thing to find a comfortable job and get kitted out in a general's uniform, but quite another to lead men, particularly in a criminal clan. For that, His Majesty the son-in-law had neither the willpower, nor the experience, nor the ability.[147]

The mafia therefore represents a mortal danger to the Party. Not only is it well organised, but it knows how to play the nationalist card. Charges of corruption levelled at Party bosses are always coupled with accusations of 'ideological laxity', with toleration of 'nationalist' or 'religious' tendencies, and their downfall is immediately followed by purges in the local Academies. The Kazakh writer, O. Suleimenov, disgraced for a time after the fall of Kunayev (the longstanding head of the Kazakh Party, whose downfall in December 1986 precipitated the Alma-Ata riots), was accused of having been in league with the ex-director of a meat consortium in Alma-Ata who had been arrested for embezzlement. In Kirghizia, the publishing industry had been completely 'privatised', and was a good source of 'unearned income' for the First Party Secretary of the Republic. It is likely that, under the circumstances, the local publishing house was producing works other than the classics of Marxism–Leninism. The cultural climate in Kirghizia must in any case have been worrying Moscow, as evidenced by the unprecedented installation of a Slav, N. Lavenov, as President of the Kirghiz Academy of Sciences.[148]

The case of Kirghizia is particularly edifying. Under cover of *glasnost* and the campaign against bureaucratisation, the federal press launched a series of attacks against local Party leaders, reproving them in particular for their tolerance of religion and the nepotism entrenched in the area. In replying to the attacks, the local interested parties, far from 'self-criticism', implied that the journalists should mind their own business. The local intelligentsia sided squarely with the officials. And, in a supreme snub to Moscow's perestroik-ist zeal, the ex-First Party Secretary, Usubaliev, sacked in 1985 and expelled from the Party for corruption (he was the enterprising publisher), was received back into the Party in 1988.[148]

The lavishing of Communist honours on mafiosi by their henchmen showed up the farcical nature of the honours themselves. In Uzbekistan 'everything was for sale – honours, dachas, Party membership cards, places at Presidiums and in cemetery plots, official positions and mandates. . . .' In Uzbekistan Rachidov proclaimed himself a 'major writer' and made his Interior Minister, Yakhaiev, a 'poet of the people'.[150] But while parodying Communist power, the mafia could also defend itself against it. Rachidov even succeeded in getting rid of the KGB leaders in Uzbekistan.[151] Gangrene had completely taken over the Party's shooting arm. Instead of trying to restore law and order, the Minister of the Interior at the time, Shchelokov –

later sacked by Andropov – embarked on the profitable project of diverting police-confiscated goods, which should have gone to the state, into special shops where his MVD (Ministry of the Interior) functionaries could buy them at a tenth of official prices. The police force itself was thus transformed into a well-organised mafia network. Mafia feudalism, in full Communist dress, could be seen to be encroaching on socialism. The gangster was handing down the law to the bureaucrat. At that point the latter was seized with nostalgia for the rule of law. The Soviet press accordingly began to publish epic pieces on the exploits of heroic pro-secutors, who at the nadir of the 'period of stagnation' (the official term for the Brezhnev era) dared do battle with the hydra of corruption, sometimes at the risk of their lives, always to the detriment of their careers. These titans are now hailed as the pioneers of *perestroika*.

Until Andropov the Soviet regime recognised only one threat to its power – dissidence and political opposition. After 1983 it began to realise that an even more serious danger was looming. As has been seen, the whole population, from children to pensioners, was liable to infection by the underworld.[152] Everywhere, Party organisations were reduced to shadows of their former selves, if not actually taken over by the more vigorous mafia networks. Contamination by the mafia was leading the Party to submerge itself in the main body of society, instead of remaining separate as the directing force of society, and to develop personal economic interests. In short, the Party seemed at risk of becoming a class in the Marxist sense: that is, a representative of certain economic interests. This process of Party 'gansterisation' has been identified as the main peril by Gorbachev and his fellow-Leninists. To combat it, they had to seek any ally, even formerly-persecuted intellectuals. The entire Party is also having to undergo a painful period of self-examination, as there can be no question of the problem being a purely regional one.

'This phenomenon has occured at national level', stated *Pravda*, in an inquiry into the roots of corruption. It published the comments of an Uzbek official indicated for misappropriation:

They made me Director of the regional sector for agricultural machinery. For two years I fought a useless battle. No way to get machinery or spare parts. What could I do? My assistant, who knew the score, said 'grease this and that person's palm'. I did it, for the first time in my life. Everything suddenly changed, like a fairy tale: it started raining spare parts.

Another Uzbek in detention added:

No one has the right to refuse a bribe. A refusal is taken as half a betrayal. Refusal to grease a palm is a 100 per cent betrayal. They hound you out of your job, expel you from the Party, they could kill you. . . . We had a strict rule. Never appoint anyone but your own to a responsible position.[153]

This last remark explains why the mafia networks could easily have taken over the Party: their principles of co-optation are the same. This is the main motive that led the Party to 'democratisation'.

NOTES

1. 3 January 1986.
2. *Pravda*, 18 June 1987.
3. *Literaturnaya Gazeta (LG)*, 17 February 1988.
4. *Moscow News*, 10 July 1988.
5. *Pravda*, 3 August 1988.
6. *LG*, 5 October 1988.
7. *Pravda*, 30 May 1988.
8. *Pravda*, 5 August 1987.
9. *LG*, 13 April 1988.
10. *Pravda*, 22 July 1988.
11. *Moscow News*, 21 August 1988.
12. *Pravda*, 4 June 1988.
13. *Pravda*, 24 September 1987.
14. XIXth CPSU Conference.
15. *LG*, 31 August 1988.
16. *Radio Liberty Research Bulletin*, 28 October 1987.
17. 9 January 1986.
18. *RLRB*, 2 September 1986.
19. *LG*, 1 April 1987.
20. *RLRB*, 7 October 1987.
21. *Izvestia*, 28 August 1985.
22. 25 January 1987.
23. *RLRB*, 19 August 1987.
24. *Izvestia*, 31 October 1985.
25. *Sovietskaya Rossiya*, 7 January 1989.
26. *LG*, 14 August 1985.
27. S. Chouprinin: 'The ladies' tango', in *LG*, 1 January 1985.
28. 17 October 1987.
29. *RLRB*, 28 September 1988.
30. XIXth CPSU Conference.
31. *Pravda*, 17 October 1987.
32. *Pravda*, 14 August 1988.
33. *Sovietskaya Rossiya*, 7 January 1989.
34. *LG*, 1 April 1987.
35. 3 January 1988.
36. *Pravda*, 13 August 1987.
37. *LG*, 3 December 1986.
38. *ibid.*
39. *Pravda*, 20 May 1988.
40. *LG*, 31 August 1988.
41. XIXth CPSU Conference

42. *LG*, 12 August 1987.
43. *RLRB*, 7 October 1987.
44. *RLRB*, 12 October 1988.
45. *RLRB*, 10 June 1987.
46. *LG*, 3 September 1986.
47. *LG*, 17 December 1986.
48. *Pravda*, 3 June 1987.
49. *LG*, 29 October 1986, 17 December 1986.
50. *LG*, 26 November 1986; *RLRB*, 14 October 1987; *Pravda*, 13 August 1988
51. *LG*, 12 October 1988.
52. *Pravda*, 13 April 1987.
53. *RLRB*, 7 October 1987.
54. *LG*, 6 May 1987.
55. *Pravda*, 19 August 1987.
56. *Pravda*, 27 November 1987.
57. XIXth CPSU Conference.
58. *Pravda*, 28 September 1987.
59. *LG, 3 February 1988.*
60. *Pravda*, 23 June 1988.
61. *Pravda*, 10 August 1987, 10 June 1988.
62. *LG*, 15 April 1987.
63. *RLRB* , 4 November 1987.
64. *Moscow News*, 17 July 1988.
65. *Pravda*, 13 April 1987.
66. *LG*, 15 April 1987.
67. 16 September 1987.
68. *Pravda*, 15 October 1987.
69. *LG*, 22 May 1985.
70. *Pravda*, 25 August 1987.
71. *LG*, 3 February 1988.
72. *RLRB*, 14 October 1987.
73. *LG*, 21 August 1985.
74. *Pravda*, 15 February 1987, 14 June 1988.
75. *Pravda*, 29 June 1987.
76. *RLRB*, 28 October 1987.
77. *RLRB*, 11 December 1985; *Pravda*, 14 June 1988.
78. *RLRB*, 14 October 1987.
79. XIXth CPSU Conference.
80. *Pravda*, 18 May 1987.
81. *RLRB*, 18 March 1987.
82. *Trud*, 12 January 1989.
83. *RLRB*, 23 September 1987.
84. 19 September 1987.
85. *Pravda*, 4 July 1988.
86. M. Gorbachev, Speech to the Plenum, June 1987.
87. 13 November 1985.
88. *RLRB*, 25 November 1987.
89. *RLRB*, 23 December 1987.
90. *RLRB*, 24 June 1987.

91. *Moskovskaya Pravda*, 4 January 1989.
92. *LG*, 3 December 1986.
93. *LG*, 4 November 1987.
94. *LG*, 16 December 1987; *Pravda*, 22 November 1987.
95. *Pravda*, 27 May 1988.
96. *RLRB*, 19 August 1988.
97. *LG*, 14 October 1987.
98. *Pravda*, 19 September 1987.
99. *LG*, 27 July 1988.
100. *LG*, 18 November 1987.
101. *ibid.*
102. *Pravda*, 19 September 1987.
103. 28 September 1987.
104. *LG*, 3 February 1988.
105. *LG*, 17 August 1988.
106. *Pravda*, 23 June 1988.
107. *Cahiers du Samizdat*, no. 129, p. 29.
108. *RLRB*, 6 July 1988.
109. *RLRB*, 17 February 1988.
110. *RLRB*, 26 August 1987.
111. *LG*, 18 March 1987.
112. *Pravda*, 1 June 1987.
113. *International Herald Tribune*, 30 December 1987.
114. *Pravda*, 5 February 1988.
115. *Pravda*, 1 June 1987, 4 July 1988.
116. *Quotidien du Médecin*, 2 May 1988.
117. State *samizdat* is semi-official material which somehow or other appears in the West.
118. *Strana y Mir*, no. 4, 1987, p. 40.
119. *LG*, 24 July 1985.
120. 18 May 1987.
121. *LG*, 12 October 1988; *RLRB*, 31 August 1988.
122. See *Ogonyok*, no. 5, 1987, and *Pensée Russe*, 13 March 1988.
123. *Pravda*, 23 June 1988.
124. *RLRB*, 9 March 1988.
125. *International Herald Tribune*, 15 February 1989.
126. *ibid.*
127. *Medicinskaya Gazeta*, 18 January 1989.
128. *LG*, 1 July 1985.
129. *Izvestia*, 19 January 1989.
130. See *Pravda*, 17 August and 21 July 1988.
131. *RLRB* , 13 February 1985.
132. *RLRB*, 19 August 1987.
133. *Le Monde*, 10 February 1989.
134. *Sovietskaya Kultura*, 14 January 1989.
135. XIXth CPSU Conference.
136. *Moscow News*, 24 April 1988.
137. 7 January 1989.
138. *LG*, 20 January 1988.

139. No. 6, 1986, pp. 36–40.
140. 17 July 1988.
141. 14/16 February 1986.
142. For mafias, see *LG*, 20 July 1988 and 17 August 1988; *Pravda*, 23 January 1988.
143. *Pravda*, 17 July 1988.
144. *LG*, 17 August 1988.
145. *ibid.*
146. *Pravda*, 23 January 1988.
147. 30 August 1988.
148. *RLRB*, 13 May 1987 and 15 July 1987.
149. *RLRB*, 20 July 1988.
150. *Moscow News*, 3 April 1988.
151. *ibid.*
152. In Solzhenitsyn's *Gulag Archipelago* there is an interesting reflection on the contamination of Soviet society by thuggery: 'While the regime was trying (or not trying) to re-educate inmates with slogans, the inmates were re-educating the area around the Archipelago. The camp lessons in brutality, cruelty, hard-heartedness, and hatred of good work were quickly learnt in the immediate vicinity and from there spread throughout the country. This was the Archipelago's revenge on the land which had created it'.
153. *Pravda*, 17 July 1988.

2. The state of the economy

The black picture of the economy emerging under *glasnost* is literally overwhelming, even in the version given by the official press: 'The state is broke. The three great reforms (1957, 1965, 1979) were failures.'[1] The Soviet economy is 'centralised anarchy'.[2] 'Under the formal dictatorship of the Plan, the economy is growing more and more anarchic.'[3]

Not one of 170 essential production sectors has fulfilled the objectives of the Plan a single time over the last 20 years . . . this has brought about a chain reaction of hardship and imbalance which has led to 'planned anarchy'. And this state of affairs has provided the objective pretext for a chain reaction of alterations to the Plan, in an attempt to face the real situation. To make things worse, each year billions of roubles have been put in circulation for the purchase of goods which never appeared, which has increased the gap between money and available goods . . . the disequilibrium has affected every pore of our economy, and has become legendary.[4]

The tyranny of the Plan and the artificial fixing of prices (many lower than the cost of the raw materials) have bred an Economy of the Absurd in which it is in the interest of enterprises to produce as little as possible with the maximum labour and resources. If the Plan is ever fulfilled on time or at least before the fixed deadline, the collective receives a bonus. The director of the collective therefore goes to massive effort to ensure that the requirements he has to meet are as low as possible, and he will move mountains not to exceed them in case the overfulfilment should be noticed and the subsequent targets raised by the Ministry. Furthermore, as production often grinds to a halt altogether because of non-delivery of raw materials, the director engages surplus staff to work overtime when the goods finally arrive (especially as his own benefits depend on the number of workers under his command). Naturally, production quality suffers, and fear of shortages leads to the hoarding of raw materials: 'Stock hoarded at enterprise depots has reached a value of 470 billion roubles, about 50 per cent of the gross national product.'[5]

Overcentralisation is likewise at the root of many absurdities. The Centre dictates the smallest details: a biscuit factory in the Baltic states must use receipes laid down in Moscow. Other problems are the almost universal non-qualification of workers, drunkenness in the workplace, antiquated equipment, lack of mechanisation, unreliable transport, losses during delivery, petrol shortages, frequently deplorable working conditions, general waste of resources, environmental pollution and dissipation of investments. At present there are at least 350,000 enterprises under construction, and the number of building projects is always climbing.

Though the planned Soviet economy concentrates on the means of production to the detriment of consumer goods, it is unable to keep up to date. In 1929, 60.5 per cent of industrial production went on the 'B' sector (consumer goods); in 1940, the figure had fallen to 39 per cent, in 1960 to 27.5 per cent, in 1986 to 24.7 per cent. The priority given by Gorbachev to the machine-building sector did nothing to reverse the decline – just the opposite.[6] Even in the unlikely event that productivity was increased, it would not help, because the economy would still continue to function for its own sake, destroying resources and the environment without benefit to the population.

The black economy has already been described, but the state economy itself has spawned a whole underground network, the only means of relieving the burdens of the bureaucratic machine. Directors organise exchanges between enterprises, establishing a system of mutual favours: 'Groups form of people who are employed in different organisations and administrations, formally independent of each other, but in reality bound in continuing close relationships. These groups are informal; their motivations, composition and behaviour are uncontrollable; their influence on the state economy is immense.'[7] This proliferation of unofficial links has contributed as much as the parallel economy to the weakening of the grip of central power.

Glasnost has revealed that the state of the national budget is less bright than had formerly been suggested. The USSR lost 66 billion dollars when petrol prices fell. Twenty-four thousand enterprises are running at a loss. In 1988 the national deficit was 36 billion roubles.[8] Other Soviet sources give a more likely figures which is three times higher. From 1985 to 1988 the national revenue increased by 1.9 billion roubles, while spending increased by 74 billion.[9]

Agriculture is in an even more catastrophic condition. The director of a collective farm (kolkhoz) has the same worries as his counterpart in industry (i.e. ensuring that the Plan's targets do not ruin his kolkhoz, reconciling totally unrealistic objectives laid down from above with the scant means at his disposal). But he has even less room to manoeuvre. He has no right to choose his crops. The authorities decide everything – what, where and when to plant, when to harvest, and so forth. The main problem is how to keep rural people in the country. The life there offers no attractions for the young: 40 per cent of dwellings are run down;[10] most have no running water, many have no electricity; the isolation of villages is made worse by the lack of roads.

In fact, the countryside is emptying: the Pskov region, for instance, has lost a quarter of its inhabitants over the last 12 years, and there are plans to ship Daghestanis in to lease abandoned areas.[11] There are 725,000 abandoned houses in the Soviet countryside, 500,000 of these in the RSFSR. In kolkhozes and sovkhozes 500,000 tractors and farm machines are rusting away because of lack of manpower and 60,000 rural schools have been

closed over the last 20 years, mostly in the RSFSR.[12] Since May 1982 the
Komsomol has regularly despatched young people into the country in the
hope that they will remain there: 600,000 young people have been sent to
kolkhozes to help with livestock (400,000 in the RSFSR). But most of them
return to the city at the first opportunity.[13] For the past few years harvest
time has required a virtual mass mobilisation of city-dwellers to the
accompaniment of panic-stricken media campaigns. In September 1988
Moscow News was calling for 'a total mobilisation of available strength and
resources to speed up the harvest' and 'a wider appeal for seasonal help'.[14] In
1987 700,000 schoolchildren and teachers were called up for the cotton
harvest.[15] It can be imagined how much disruption this causes in work and
in transportation (buses must be requisitioned to take all these people to the
fields). Notwithstanding all these efforts, the kolkhoz often cannot use the
huge urban reinforcements as work is brought to a halt because of broken-
down machinery or fuel shortages.

In 1988 the official media revealed figures for agriculture which painted
an even blacker picture than had been imagined in the West. Half the grain
consumed in the USSR is imported.[16] From 1985 to 1987 the Soviet Union
spent more than 23 billion roubles on imported staple foods.[17] Meanwhile,
the state spends 23–5 billion roubles on the kolkhozes each year and 50
million on the sovkhozes.[18] It appears that the rosy grain statistics of the
Brezhnev era were overestimates, as harvest figures included weeds, rocks
and whatnot. The true figure was often 10 per cent lower than given, or even
30 per cent.[19] A third of agricultural products never reach the consumer;[20]
25–30 per cent is lost in storage or transport at the best of times.[21] Only 28
per cent of potatoes delivered to Moscow actually reach the table.[22] As the
media point out, a Soviet cow gives about as much milk as an American
goat. Livestock diseases and weight loss while cattle queue for slaughter
cause the loss of over a million tonnes of meat a year.[23] The agricultural
processing industry, which employrs 4 million people, is breaking down.[24]

Other symptoms show the extent of the mess. The agricultural decline has
not only affected the state sector, but also the small number of officially-
permitted individual plots. Many farmers, discouraged by constant
difficulties and with fingers burnt by previous experience, are no longer
bothering to raise their permitted individual quota of cattle. There are only
50 or 60 cows per 100 families.[25] In 1967, there were 29.2 million cows raised
by individuals. In 1980, there were fewer than 23.1 million. Lack of fodder is
a constant complaint, causing people to slaughter their livestock. The
shortage of farm equipment, particularly small tractors, also discourages the
collective farmer from making the most of what he is allowed to raise on his
own.

There has been a media outcry about the ravages brought about by 'land
improvement'. In Central Asia 'deserts are turning into swamps before our
eyes, which has no precedent in the history of irrigation.'[26] Incompetent
irrigation is raising the level of salt in the soil, making it unfit for cultivation;

20–40 per cent of the famous Chernozium region has been ruined in this way.[27] The decline worsened throughout 1987: the number of cattle decreased by 2 million head, as against a decrease of 400,000 in 1986 – in both the state and individual sectors.[28] Over the 11th five-year Plan, the average annual harvest decreased by 14 per cent.

Until now, the Soviet economy has been based on the requisition principle: the state appropriates most goods produced in factories and kolkhozes and oversees their distribution as far as it can, which is not far, to judge by the empty shops. 'Provincials' are thus obliged to go to Moscow to buy meat produced in their own area: each year, 760,000 tonnes of meat are 'exported' from the capital in this way. The Kalinin region, for instance, sends 38,000 tonnes of meat to Moscow, where Kalinin residents buy back almost half. The state of the meat after all this time-consuming toing and froing may be imagined.[29]

The anti-alcohol campaign highlighted the problems of the Soviet economy. Enterprises found themselves with no cash to pay employees, as only the sale of vodka maintains currency circulation.[30] Soviet economists are hoping to substitute a system of taxes for state requisitioning of goods, arguing that capitalist governments enjoy much better means of exercising economic leverage than does the CPSU, and that in fact the planned economy has led to such chaos that the Soviet central authorities have lost all control over the state economy. High-level initiatives simply disappear into the maze of the bureaucratic apparatus and its 'parallel' networks.

NOTES

1. *LG*, 18 May 1988.
2. *LG*, 4 May 1988.
3. *Moscow News*, 8 May 1988.
4. *Pravda*, 30 May 1988.
5. *Moscow News*, 20 November 1988.
6. See the interview with V. Seiounin in *Pensée Russe*, 26 February 1988.
7. T. Zaslavskaya, quoted in *Possev*, no. 3, March 1988, p. 25.
8. *International Herald Tribune*, 28 October 1988.
9. Gorbachev, speech to the Council of Ministers, 20 November 1988.
10. *Pravda*, 5 December 1987.
11. *Pravda*, 11 July 1988.
12. *Pravda*, 30 August 1988.
13. *Communist of the Armed Forces*, no. 7, April 1988.
14. 11 September 1988.
15. *LG*, 16 March 1988.
16. *LG*, 13 April 1988.
17. *LG*, 28 September 1988.
18. *LG*, 3 August 1988.
19. *LG*, 11 May 1988.

20. *LG*, 21 October 1987.
21. *LG*, 14 August 1988.
22. *Moscow News*, 20 November 1988.
23. *Pravda*, 6 July 1988.
24. *Pravda*, 19 October 1987.
25. *LG*, 18 November 1987.
26. *Pravda*, 7 July 1988.
27. *Pravda*, 17 June 1988.
28. *LG*, 11 May 1988.
29. *ibid.*
30. *Moscow News*, 10 July 1988 and *Pravda*, 1 September 1988.

3. *Perestroika*

The whole of Gorbachev's domestic policy has been conceived in response to the crisis outlined in the first chapter. The regime originally thought it could solve the country's problems by the usual methods of communism: repression and campaigns for discipline, decrees and firmer control. However, the classic Leninist remedies did nothing but aggravate the situation, and the Party reached the painful conclusion that the traditional practices had nothing more to offer. It was necessary to look elsewhere. *Perestroika* can be divided into two periods: the 'Andropovian' period, from 1985-6, when 'discipline' and 'order' were the slogans of the day after the lapses of the Brezhnev era; and a second period which could be called the period of 'disarray' – during which the regime had to improvise desperate attempts to revive, without making any major political concessions, a society frozen in indifference or hostility.

GLASNOST

Why did the Soviet regime take the risk of *glasnost*? Several motives account for its adoption of this new policy toward intellectuals and the media.

First, there was the desire to recapture the ideological territory lost under Brezhnev and to take the offensive in this area, both at home and abroad. According to the formula of A. Yakovlev, one of the architects of *glasnost*,

The world today is growing ever smaller from the point of view of communication, and more interdependent. To imagine that it is possible to create in this world a refuge or cloister cut off from outside influence, and to remain there passively, is not only to indulge in illusion but to condemn oneself to defeat. We need to be active ourselves, to take an offensive that will not only guarantee us absolute priority in our own house but will systematically reinforce our influence in the outside world.

Glasnost was introduced to neutralise Western influence in two ways: first by taking away the West's monopoly of exclusive news stories about the USSR ('It is enough for us to overtake the West in order to disarm it immediately'[1]). 'It is stupid to hide from people what is in any case utterly impossible to disguise.'[2] Furthermore, *glasnost* aimed to enlist the Western media in the service of Soviet propaganda by bombarding them with rumours and sensations which they then hastened to broadcast both in the West and to the Communist Block. Thanks to *glasnost*, the West is losing interest in the Soviet opposition, preferring to fix its attention on the intrigues within the Politburo and the conflict between the 'conservatives' and Gorbachev and his allies. In other words, the regime has practically won back the monopoly of information about the USSR taken from it by the dissidents in the 1970s.

Thanks to *glasnost*, Soviet ideologists can now frame the terms of tghe debate about reform not only at home but in the West, imposing notions of 'bureaucratic resistance', 'conservatives putting the brakes on *perestroika*', 'new thinking', 'distortions of socialism', and so forth. And this New Look sovspeak is obligingly disseminated in the democratic countries by Western radio, neutralising at least for a while the effect that the actual revelations of *glasnost* must otherwise have had. E. Primakov sums this up perfectly; for him *glasnost* is 'an essential means of influencing public opinion, at home and in the West'.[3]

The second main reason for the adoption of *glasnost* is linked to the need to 'organise the initiative of the masses':

We must and will transform the press . . . from a simple tool for political communication or for the battle against bourgeois lies into a weapon of economic re-education for the masses, a weapon which will bring home to the masses the necessity of working to a new pattern . . . the introduction of *glasnost* into this area will indeed be an enormous reform and will serve to encourage the masses to take upon themselves the solution to the problems which affect them most.

This comment is not from Gorbachev but from Lenin, and was made in March 1918.[4]

Another no less Leninist motive prompted the launching of *glasnost*. *Glasnost* is meant to be 'one of the forms of social control',[5] a means for the central authorities to keep an eye on the activities of local cadres and of denouncing the 'adversaries of *perestroika*', i.e. those not toeing the Party line. 'The people know all . . . they can see all that stands in the way of *perestroika*.'[6] *Glasnost* is 'a means óf mass control of Party activity and of all the organs of power'.[7] It plays a central role in the Gorbachev offensive against backsliding Party officials and in the Party's battle to regain real power at the heart of Soviet society. *Glasnost* has set itself against 'formalism' – that barrier of deception, rigged statistics, false records, and reports of imaginary achievements that constitutes the population's usual protection against the incessant incursions of the Party.

The Gorbachev team also understood to what extent it was necessary to woo the intellectuals, for reasons of domestic and foreign policy. At home, the Party needed a 'secondary consciousness' to distract attention from its new offensive on society, this time in the name of economic efficiency. *Glasnost* has not only revealed selected facts, but successfully won over the intelligentsia, cutting it off from popular awareness and driving a wedge between intellectuals and the rest of the population. The experience of Solidarnosc, where the Communist regime was imperilled by an alliance between workers and intellectuals, has been taken into account. As Sinyavsky emphasised during his visit to the USSR in January 1989, 'the absence of sausage in the shops is substantially compensated by the new possibility of reading Nabokov and Pasternak in Soviet editions'. Sinyavsky's remarks have provoked criticism from some dissidents, which shows some awareness of the dangers of the authorities' present policy.

Finally, *glasnost* was launched as a watershed, a breaking-point between the old order and the new era of *perestroika* at a time when 'the well of popular confidence had run dry'.[8] It was introduced to induce the Soviet people and those in the non-Communist world, to forget past experience of communism and renew their cooperation with the regime as though nothing untoward had ever occurred, as though its admission of former crimes was an argument in its favour. It is no mean feat for Soviet propaganda to have transformed the bloody history of the Communist regime into an advertisement for the Party. Imagine the Germans, had they remained under Nazi domination, publishing accounts of the Holocaust in order to promote a '*perestroika* in international relations' to their advantage.

Like *perestroika*, *glasnost* already has a history which makes for interesting study. For some time at first, the press embarked on a mission to explore the Augean stables of Soviet society, taking note of the social ills left over from the Brezhnev era. This parade of evils included the breakdown in public health and morals, alcoholism, drugs, prostitution, flaws in the economy, the corruption of bureaucracy (especially in the republics), the black economy, the problems of pollution, and so forth. There was no mention throughout the first phase of any possible political implication in the revelations. In 1987, however, the idea was put forward that the economic difficulties might be linked to political causes, and little by little examination of the regime's past has assumed precedence over everything else. There was was an outbreak of attacks on Stalin but the focus soon shifted from the man himself to the question of what made the 'cult of personality' possible. Since April 1988 the last remaining sacred cows of the Stalin era have been sacrificed. Numerous articles appeared demonstrating that collectivisation had absolutely no economic justification, as slave labour (the word is used) is not profitable; that Stalin was responsible for enormous and wasteful loss of life during the Second World War, and that the Hitler–Stalin Pact was – worse than a crime – a mistake. The word 'totalitarianism' caught on immediately in the USSR, as opposed to the West where it encountered fierce resistance from 'liberal' Sovietologists, especially in the USA. The Stalin chapter was hardly closed before the Soviet press moved on to Brezhnev, who is now being accused of having done the country just as much harm, albeit in a milder way. Brezhnev, it is said, broke down the moral fibre of the population and sowed cynicism, corruption and careerism.

The media, in short, are now presenting Soviet history as a 'chain of errors and crimes', to borrow Ligachev's phrase; and at times even Lenin himself does not appear immune from the 'explosion of *glasnost*' (another of the 'conservatives'' expressions). It has been said for instance that the USSR has never been a law-based state and that the first phase of communism (under Lenin) contained the seeds of Stalinism. For the moment, Lenin is still a 'protected zone', however, and the Leninist roots of the system cannot be touched upon except indirectly.

Of course, such unmasking is fraught with ideological peril (though the effect of *glasnost* here should not be exaggerated: the greater part of ideological disaffection occurred in the late 1960s and early 1970s). It may be assumed that the Party would never have embarked upon it without a number of 'fire-breaks', including the following:

•Skilful manipulation of sovspeak: a whole series of buffer phrases, beyond which it is inadvisable to venture, have been laid down by Gorbachev's think tanks. Among these are: 'braking mechanisms' (given as explanation for all lack of improvement these last three years); 'bureaucracy' (the Party); 'the system of administrative command' (the Communist system); 'distortions of socialism' (implying that there is an alternative, 'proper' socialism), and above all, *'perestroika'* itself, sovspeak term *par excellence*, the meaning of which may be, and is, arbitrarily decided by the Party.
•Organisation of decoy debates and the trotting out of opinion whipped up on bogus issues: e.g. great agitation over the proposed design of monuments, preservation of historic buildings, repatriation of Soviet troops held prisoner in Pakistan, and so forth. In this respect, nationalism can be valuable: it is preferable to have intellectuals clashing over the question of whether the Jews and Freemasons are the root of all Russia's ills, whether rock music perverts the young, or whether nude women should appear on screen, than to open press columns to a debate on whether communism can or cannot be reformed.

In the main, *glasnost* has done nothing to reduce the Russian and Soviet parochialism which helps maintain the grip of ideology on the public mind (a grip due less to Leninist dogma than to the persistence of thought-patterns conditioned by ideology, such as idolatry of national culture, denunciation of modernity, and so forth). The Gorbachev thaw has hatched out numerous literary works frozen under the former leadership, but all Russian and Soviet, not foreign. However gifted, they do nothing to open the mind. They give the critics a chance to display fine feelings and re-hash questions thrashed out a hundred times, such as 'humanism' in art or 'sincerity' in writing. They also provide an excellent opportunity to settle scores with those dinosaurs of the Writers' Union who prospered under Brezhnev. There is little genuine literary criticism and even less political philosophy, two genres constantly mixed and consequently both destroyed. One way of breaking the stranglehold on the development of thought could be study of foreign classics far removed from Russian and Soviet tradition and problems. When will Soviet reviewers plunge into Aristotle and Locke,

Tocqueville and Benjamin Constant with the same energy they devote to exhuming second-rate Russian philosophers? *Glasnost* has given people fetishes of possibly symbolic value but no real content. Now as before, idolatry and the quarrels of the idolaters occupy the whole intellectual scene, much to the satisfaction of the Party.

Each writer is now obliged to advertise his allegiance to one of the two camps set up by *glasnost*: the so-called 'liberal' and 'conservative' camps, each of which has its own literary idols – those authors resuscitated by the Gorbachev thaw for the liberals, and anti-Western, patriotic, 'Russian' authors for the conservatives. It would be a mistake to see this virulent but artificial opposition as the beginning of a real political life in the Soviet Union or as an embryonic stage of the Western split between Left and Right, as Soviet propaganda would have us believe. It should be remembered that the 'liberal' Rybakov launched a violent attack in the 'progressive' *Moscow News* on those who wanted to add some names from the 1920s to a 'memorial to the victims of repression'. The 'conservative' author Soloukhin, on the other hand, explained in the 'nationalist' review *Nash Sovremennik* his refusal to join the memorial association on the grounds that it commemorated only Stalin's victims, leaving out the victims of Lenin's Red Terror, which he described in vivid terms. Contrary to Sinyavsky's claims[9] the opposition between Communists and anti-Communists is more relevant than ever. It is this opposition that the Soviet regime fears, and is trying to conceal behind the spectacle of 'liberalism' vs. 'conservatism'.

There is, however, some hope that this climate may not be permanent. If the lies and the fear recede, it will be increasingly difficult for the authorities to continue channelling intellectual life into a safe dead-end. With increased access to reality, the Soviets will rediscover thought. Even today there are signs of it in the articles of some economists – who are more than any other Soviet intellectuals exposed to 'socialism in practice'. It is their writings which contain the real seeds of an articulate political analysis.

Has an increase in press freedom accompanied the decrease in lies? Has the Party withdrawn completely from the media sphere? Media behaviour in times of crisis gives some idea of the true value of *glasnost*. Whenever taken by surprise by some unexpected serious event, the press has maintained a cautious silence or given a brief report while waiting for instructions from the top on how to proceed. This was the case with the Alma-Ata and Soumgait riots and also with Chernobyl. Regular reading of the press shows that, even on less critical occasions, there is a prompter in the wings. Identical campaigns have been launched in various journals at the same time: identical themes appear simultaneously in similar organs; the same authors come back into favour at the same time in different literary reviews; there is the feeling that the cue has been given from above to lift another taboo. *Glasnost* ebbs and flows, with daring ventures followed by retreats into orthodoxy and primitive sovspeak. All these vicissitudes are doubtless linked to political infighting hidden from the West, and to the party's disarray in the face of a situation which is getting out of hand. They prove one thing, at any rate: up to now, despite increasing pressures from below, the press remains an instrument of the regime. Gorbachev is continually reminding media representatives that 'criticism must always be made in the spirit of the Party'.[10] In January 1988 one of the 'pioneers' of *glasnost*, V. Korotich, editor of the review *Ogonyok*, declared: 'When *Ogonyok* publishes articles on historical figures, it is careful to avoid questions which are in the sole jurisdiction of Party organs.' E. Yakovlev, Editor-in-Chief of *Moscow News*, another leading organ of *glasnost* (though intended mainly for export, as it is extremely difficult for Soviet citizens to get hold of it), says: 'I continue to believe that our Party has the right to decide what must and must not be published.'[11] Only time will tell whether *glasnost* will acquire its own momentum.

THE FIRST STAGE OF *PERESTROIKA*

The launch of *perestroika* was marked by the introduction of the Law Against Unearned Income, the gospriomka and the anti-alcohol campaign. These measures were the culmination of the Andropov campaign for order and discipline.

The Law Against Unearned Income, adopted in May 1986, aimed to destroy the parallel economy. Its goal is prosecution of all those with income not derived from official employment and all those engaged in unregistered professional activity. The ideal is to channel the energies expended on the parallel economy back into the state. The second Party salvo against the black economy was the legalising (in November 1986) of 'individual professional activity', and the law on cooperatives (more on this later). The state was thus taking steps to control everything it did not forbid outright.

The creation of the gospriomka reveals the basic philosophy of Gorbachevism and highlights the discrepancy between all the speeches in favour of 'market socialism' and the real practices of the regime. The gospriomka is a state commission independent of the enterprises, responsible for quality control. It is empowered to carry out inspections and to reject unsatisfactory products. The enterprise concerned (and its workers) bear any consequent loss. The idea was first introduced in military production, and afterwards transferred to the civilian sector. As Gorbachev says: 'I do not want to paint too black a picture. There are things that we do well. Take defence: in this area, we are second to none. But there, the controllers, I must say, command total respect: from workers, engineers, designers and officials. That is how the gospriomka must operate.'[12] The new commission was designed to oversee the 'technical controls' already in existence, which were carried out by the enterprises' own staff. There are still 10 million of these 'people's controllers'.

In the battle against alcohol, Gorbachev has gone much further than his predecessors. The price of alcoholic beverages increased by 15–25 per cent in 1985, and by a further 20–5 per cent in 1986. In 1986–7 the production of vodka and wine fell by 32 per cent and 68 per cent respectively. In 1987 sales of alcohol continued to drop – by 20 per cent from the 1986 figure.[13] Many liquor stores have been closed. In 1985 the procedure for putting alcoholics into detoxification centres was greatly simplified. Previously, they would need to have been guilty of 'repeated infractions of workplace discipline, of public order, of the rules of socialist life'. From now on, they need only be declared chronic alcoholics. This has tripled the number of drunkards sent to 'places of prophylactic work therapy' (LTPs). These first appeared in the mid 1960s, under the control of the Ministry of the Interior. In the early 1980s there were 300 of them in all; 100–150,000 people were detained in them, cut off from the world outside. They are patterned on the gulag, with barracks, watchtowers, guards and forced labour. The doctors are MVD officials. The forced cure lasts at least 18 months, and can be prolonged a the request of the police 'psychiatrist'. The old network of LTPs was judged wholly inadequate, and a Council of Ministers decree anticipated the construction of new and larger LTPs betwen 1986 and 1990.[14]

For agriculture, a new organisation – the gosagroprom – was created with the object of amalgamating the kolkhozes and the agricultural processing industry into a single unit; according to *Pravda*,[15] this was 'a new solution to the problem of urban and rural integration'.

This first stage of *perestroika* had rapid and predictable results. Bolstered by the Law Against Unearned Income, local authorities launched an assault on unfortunate kolkhozians trying to sell the meagre fruits of their 'individual plot' in the marketplace. This successfully emptied the markets without improving the state sector, and the availability of foodstaples dropped spectacularly in 1986. This same ill-conceived law also let loose a wave of depression in the commercial sector: in 1985-6,800,000 employees in this sector, sales staff and shop managers, were either arrested or left their jobs for fear of prosecution.[16] The consequences of such a rout may be imagined: ever-lengthening queues, rudeness and aggression among surviving sales staff. Other effects of the Law Against Unearned Income were: an aggravation of the housing shortage, as no one dared let rooms any more;[17] and massive overcrowding of public transport, because 'private' drivers were reluctant to accept paying passengers, as most had done previously. Itinerant contract workers (*shabashniki*) were also persecuted, much to the chagrin of the kolkhozes, which depend largely on this flexible and efficient manpower. In promulgating the law, the Soviet authorities doubtless saw it as a weapon against large-scale corruption. But the wheels of the Communist system continued to roll. The basic aim of the law was not achieved. In the best Leninist tradition, civil society suffered most from this whirlwind of administrative zeal. 'It is obvious that we have gone too far', admitted *Pravda*.[18]

The gospriomka has likewise disappointed the hopes placed in it. Now, producers simply take more trouble over goods which remain unsaleable.[19] Censured workers allege, often rightly, that poor raw materials and ancient equipment are to blame for the shoddy product. The gospriomka itself is already becoming top-heavy and corrupt, and only serves to poison the atmosphere in enterprises under threat of inspection. In the end, the inspectors just throw up their hands and approve botched goods.

Nor has the press attempted to conceal the complete failure of the gosagroprom. Since its creation, provision of machinery to kolkhozes has deteriorated.[20] In the kolkhoz/processing industry 'partnership', the kolkhoz is the weaker, falling into debt while the processing industries accumulate bonuses. Bureaucracy continues to thrive. In short, 'the current system of management of the gosagroprom has shown itself to be inefficient and outdated'.[21]

The anti-alcohol campaign induced an initial period of euphoria in the media. Lists of impressive statistics were quoted. Thanks to the anti-vodka measures, criminality, road accidents and accidents in the workplace fell by a fifth;[22] the number of deaths from cardiovascular disease dropped by 100,000.[23] Absenteeism fell by 33–40 per cent.

But before long shadows fell across the scene. In three years, losses in revenue from alcohol sales had cost the state 37 billion roubles, notwithstanding the rise in the price of alcohol. Public places were no longer full of drunks: they stayed home to drink instead, to the chagrin (and peril) of their families and neighbours. Anything at all was being drunk in the absence of vodka: eau de Cologne, hair lotion, mouthwash and various medicines which quickly disappeared from the shops. Alcoholic poisoning is now on the increase. In 1984 47,300 deaths were attributed to alcohol. In 1987 this figure had dropped to 20,000, but 40,000 cases of poisoning from vodka substitutes were counted, 11,000 of them fatal.[25] The Soviet drinker spends an average of 70 to 90 hours a year queuing for vodka. Maintaining order in these queues requires police contingents twice as large as three years ago.[26] But above all, the distilling of moonshine (*samogon*) has enjoyed a continuing boom. Traditionally a rural commodity, it is now well established in the cities. Judging from press reports, local authorities often encourage trafficking in it and the police turn a blind eye. In 1986 158,000 people were prosecuted for illicit distilling; in 1987 the figure was 500,000.[27] Second offenders are liable to up to two years' imprisonment or fines of up to 500 roubles. At present, illegal stills are producing more alcohol than the state.[28] It appears that the only brake on the *samogon* boom is the shortage of sugar. Yevtushenko attests that 'in many cases a battle against state-produced vodka is being waged, but not against alcoholism.'[29] The state has finally come to realise its weakness in this unequal combat, and the risks it incurs. 'The fight against illegal distilling threatens to degenerate into a sort of civil war, with all the "extraordinary measures" and excesses that this entails: invasion of homes, surveillance and informing, mobilisation of the forces of order', states the independent review *Glasnost*.[30] The new Temperance Societies are mocked: they get few recruits among workers, so reluctant Party members feel obliged to join. In Odessa, the police raided a still belonging to the president of the local Temperance Society.[31]

The authorities are now conscious of having committed a costly error in undertaking the assault on alcohol with traditional Communist weapons of prohibition and repression. Not only has alcoholism refused to retreat (in 1987 the number of road accidents due to drunkenness were 45 per cent higher than the previous year), but private initiative has taken great strides in the only area where *perestroika* has really stimulated the Soviets' spirit of enterprise. Illegal distilling now appears an irreversible trend:

Real life has proved that the decision concerning the fight against alcoholism was not well thought out . . . even if alcohol prices now fall, even if there is enough to go round everywhere, it will be difficult to modify the situation, as illegal distilling is now an established practice.[32]
In the final instance, we have lost a great deal, not least because the state has lost the monopoly of alcohol production.[33]

The regime is also terrified of the political consequences of the campaign. The population has taken sugar shortage very badly: 'Before, there were queues for everything, and it was all right, no one minded too much. But now that we are queuing for sugar, something has snapped, and people are beginning to be angry.'[54]

These measures outline the main features of the first stage of *perestroika*. Other decisions taken in the same spirit were: the introduction of the multi-shift system (by the Decree of 13 February 1987); the crackdown on 'parasitism' (in Moscow, for instance, the Resolution of 10 June 1986 obliges all able-bodied men to display a certificate of employment in their place of residence in order to unmask those persons evading work useful to society'[35]; and salary differentiation according to performance (Decree of 17 September 1986), which aims among other things to 'strengthen the role of the collective in the assessment of each worker's output'.[36] *Perestroika* began as a systematic attack on society skilfully disguised in rhetoric reminiscent of the new Economic Policy of the 1920s, and with enthusiastic support from intellectuals feted under *glasnost*. The true nature of this *perestroika* has entirely escaped the West, bewitched by Gorbachevian propaganda. Within the Soviet Union itself, the situation is more complex.

The intelligentsia has been divided from the population and seduced by various crumbs of freedom. The people looked favourably on the Andropovian campaign for order and discipline, as it drew largely on the illusion, maintained by Gorbachev in 1985 that the system would revive if everyone was made to work properly. All this changed when people realised that the new restrictions and punishments were not directed solely at the crooked salesman, corrupt officials and speculators but at everyone else as well: that everyone was destined to suffer from salary cuts, restrictive drinking laws and shift work. Resentment was aggravated by empty shops and markets. By 1986 the crisis was acute. The regime became aware of the danger of resorting to traditional Communist formulae demonstrating the Party's power (i.e. policies of 'prohibit and punish'). It was not enough that *glasnost* had proved more effective than the gulag at gagging a population now bombarded with Western radio programmes praising Gorbachev's reforms and marvelling at the wind of change. Most Soviets sensed a swindle in the proclamation of the 'new thinking' and recognised this *perestroika* for what it was: another manipulation by the Party of the 'human factor'; a new experiment in communism just like all the previous attempts. The people thus turned to out their own time-honoured weapon of the undeclared go-slow. The Party saw the situation becoming crucial and decided to beat a retreat. At the CPSU Plenum in February 1987, Gorbachev spoke for the first time of *perestroika* in the political system.

THE SECOND STAGE OF *PERESTROIKA*

Economic measures and their consequences
The Law on Enterprises, promulgated in July 1987, caught the West's attention with the magic words 'autonomy' and 'self-accounting' (*khozras-chet*), 'economic methods of management' and 'self-management'. All these words appear in the actual text of the law. But close analysis shows that the 'autonomy' refers to accountability of the collective – and its director – for failure, with no corresponding freedom of action. 'State orders' for goods, determined by Gosplan and the Ministries, still take priority. The enterprise has discretion only over what remains. It must obey 'control figures' and 'indexes' laid down from above. 'It is as though the directors were being forced to swim with their hands and feet tied.'[37] How can 'self-accounting' have any meaning, while prices continue to be fixed arbitrarily and the currency has no consistent value? As long as the rouble remains a fiction and not a genuine instrument of measure, there can be no significant economic reform.

It is unlikely that the planned project to regroup into several thousand state cartels the 37,000 enterprises now under ministerial control will do much to alleviate the bureaucratic burden.

As for the so-called self-management, the law says: 'The Party organisation within the enterprise is the political kernel of the collective and directs the work of the entire collective, the organs of self-management, the trade union, the Komsomol and other organisations; it controls the activities of the administration'. This shows how Gorbachevian 'democracy' must be understood. It is primarily a reactivating of grassroots Communist orga-nisations, charged with supervising workers and administration at the same time. The election of directors of enterprises by workers' collectives is being brandished as a 'superiority' of socialist democracy over bourgeois democracy. There again, the text of the law is worth examining: 'If the candidate chosen by the collective is not approved by higher authorities, new elections will be initiated'.

The Law on Enterprises falls far below the expectations raised by various previous declarations. Gosplan and Ministries remain intact, the state continues to fix prices.

In agriculture the decrees of September 1987 stipulated that the kolkhozes and the processing industry must incorporate 'self-accounting' by the end of 1989. The system of contractual work brigades should have been universally adopted in 1988 (in 1983, this was foreseen for 1985).[38] The decrees also authorise long-term leasing of land. Local authorities were charged with fixing the boundaries of individual plots and regulating private stock-rearing. Farmers now have the right to use horses and oxen for cultivation of their private plot, on condition of course that the animals are also used in the state sector. Various decrees have ensured that private agricultural production will be commercialised via state networks, which does not augur well. The idea is to divide the kolkhozes into small self-financing units 'with integration of all the fundamental links into the state sector', which represents a 'dialectical combination of the advantages of large-scale production provided by kolkhozes and sovkhozes with small-scale economic management'.[39] It is hoped simultaneously to 'responsibilise' individuals by making them bear the losses (self-accounting), while restricting individual initiative in state organisations and harnessing it to the dead weight of collective state enterprises.

In October 1987 only 280,000 citizens had the right to pursue an 'individual activity'.[40] According to the Maslov report (already quoted) the number of applications is far above what the authorities are prepared to allow:

the introduction of the law on individual activity raises problems. Forty per cent of all people of working age have applied for authorisation. For many there is a great temptation to work as little as possible in their official job and as much as possible in their individual activity, and that is understandable. The means to overcome this imbalance have not yet been found.

In legalising 'individual professional activity' and the cooperatives, the authorities hoped to integrate inactive sectors of the population into the economy, such as pensioners (there are 58 million of them in the USSR, of which 12 million continue to work), housewives, students and schoolchildren. The law of 8 June 1988 is deliberately obscure on the question of holding several jobs. Liberal in the main, the law guarantees the inviolability of cooperatives' property and the state's non-interference in their economic affairs. One significant article (absurd to the point of unenforceability and consequently not enforced) states:

The organisation of the Party within the cooperative constitutes its political centre, acting within the framework of the constitution . . . the socioeconomic conditions concerning the activity of the cooperative are elaborated and adopted by its directive organs with the participation of the workers' collective, Party organisations, trade unions and Komsomol represented therein.

The cooperative must develop its own 5-year Plan and coordinate it locally. The fiscal legislation of 14 March 1988 concerning cooperatives would have discouraged even the most enterprising. Under it, any income over 1,000 roubles a month was taxed by 70 per cent. This draconian provision was strongly criticised in the press and was subsequently abolished.

What can be said overall about the second phase of *perestroika*?

Enterprises are complaining that the 'state orders' often absorb more than 80 per cent of production (sometimes 98.5 per cent, or in effect 100 per cent of total production, particularly in respect of 'strategic raw materials' – it would be interesting to find out the proportion of state orders taken up by military production). With the Gosplan seizing all products, industrial areas are left with nothing to exchange for farm productions, and are therefore deprived in comparison to agricultural regions.[41] The law on enterprises led to a drop in the production of consumer goods which are uneconomic for the producer, especially as the now 'self-financing' shops reject anything unsaleable.[42] Enterprises have simply stopped making many articles because the Decree of November 1985 punishes poor quality by confiscating from 5 to 15 per cent of the enterprises' income.[43] This led economist Leonid Abalkin to remark: 'The modifications between Sector A and Sector B, between accumulation and consumption, were carried out in a spirit totally opposed to that defined by the 27th Congress. The state of the consumer market has worsened.'[44] Since the summer of 1988 new and unprecedented shortages have appeared in the Soviet Union: vacuum cleaners, washing machines, television sets, soap and washing powder have been unobtainable since December 1988. In some areas people are queuing for vegetable oil and matches.

Lame ducks continue to be funded at the expense of profitable enterprises. The use of 'economic norms' has enabled Ministries to 'maintain the possibility of taking means from successful enterprises for assignment to inefficient enterprises'.[45] Nearly 90 per cent of the profits of efficient enterprises are lifted in this way.[46] Without state support, directors have trouble finding raw materials and customers. An opinion poll shows that 80 per cent of directors feel that the new law gives them insufficient protection against encroachments from higher up.[47]

Self-accounting has had various and often unexpected ramifications. Now that they are having to bear losses, enterprises are beginning to object to losing their employees for a month and a half every year for potato-digging. Forced to be 'profitable' with antiquated equipment and poor materials, they are opting for the simplest solution: price increases. They are also reluctant to invest their meagre resources in scientific research: their priorities are to accommodate workers, provide nurseries, etc. Thus, self-accounting seems to be undermining another principle of *perestroika*, 'the acceleration of scientific-technical progress'; 'The gap between the scientific-technical level in the Soviet Union and the West is ever-widening'.[48] 'Self-accounting has led to no commercial improvements, owing to the shortage of goods'.[49] 'If only these drawbacks were compensated by an increase in productivity. But nothing doing: almost all figures from enterprises adopting self-accounting in 1987 were lower than the preceding year.'[50]

The relaxation of the monopoly on foreign trade has led to a proliferation of bureaucratic bodies, with each Ministry assigning itself a foreign trade section patterned on the Ministry of Foreign Trade. To leave nothing to chance, a state commission for foreign trade has also been created, as well as a new body, the General Directorate of Customs Control. The regime realised that with regard to foreign trade, the interests of the enterprises were conflicting with those of the state (enterprises were undercutting state prices).[51]

Self-management, the mini-revolution launched against the cadres, also had unforeseen effects. A letter to the editor of *Pravda* pointed out that 'The prestige of directors has fallen. Nowadays, few schoolchildren dream of choosing this profession. It has become very difficult to function because of criticism of directors from all levels.'[52] Workers would have little reason to elect exacting directors: their more likely choice would be someone lenient and 'understanding'. *Pravda* complains that in 1987 directors were allowing workers more holidays than previously.[53] Here again, the slogans of *perestroika* contradict themselves. It is impossible to launch a cultural revolution while increasing productivity at the same time. In Central Asia the election of directors has had another consequence judged highly undesirable by the central authorities: it reinforces the clan system.

The cooperative movement has already undergone many ups and downs. Cooperatives were slow to take off, as the rash person who decides to set up a cooperative or pursue an 'individual professional activity' must prepare himself for a veritable assault course of commissions and local bureaucrats in order to obtain raw materials, premises and credit. He must buy state-and machinery at prices 3–6 times higher than those paid by state enterprises.[54] If he survives this ordeal, he faces encroachments from local racketeers, without hope of police protection.[55] This touches on another problem: cooperatives face not only bureaucratic inertia, but also hostility from a population resentful of their high income. Shortages of goods in shops are attributed to their being bought up by cooperatives. Cooperatives are accused of buying raw materials at fixed state prices only to re-sell them at enormous profits. 'The development of cooperatives is the part of *perestroika* the least understood by the people. It is no use hiding the fact that there is a general frustration and envy towards those who have managed to succeed. . . . Are we in the process of creating a new social enemy?'[56] It is also said that all kinds of speculators and mafiosi are finding the cooperatives convenient for laundering money. *Pravda* notes gleefully that in the Moscow suburbs, nearly 90 per cent of those aspiring to 'individual professional activity' had previously been in trouble with the law and that shopkeepers sacked for theft and corruption were reappearing in the cooperatives.[57]

Small wonder, then, that the cooperative movement should be slow in developing. In July 1988 32,961 cooperatives had been created, employing 700,000 people.[58] In the first half of 1988 this number had already fallen somewhat due to the introduction of exorbitant taxation (imposed by the Decree of 14 March 1988). The authorities hoped that the cooperatives would provide healthy socialist competition to stimulate the state sector and would constitute 'an effective means to combat the distortions of the parallel economy . . . the monopoly situation of state enterprise and of illicit business.'[59] Instead, 'rather than complementing state organisations and providing them with competition, the cooperatives and individual activity . . . are gradually supplanting them and becoming monopolies.'[60] Furthermore, two out of three private 'entrepreneurs' are only too happy to practice illegally.[61] Why not, when registration would expose them to thousands of bureaucratic incursions, prying questions, exorbitant taxes, incessant controls? Also, the initial plan of getting pensioners and students into the work force is not being realised: pensioners make up 13 per cent, housewives 8 per cent and students 3 per cent of the staff of the cooperatives.[62] Instead, qualified people are quitting the state sector for the cooperatives. The authorities' hope that the cooperatives would improve the lot of the consumer was also dashed. The cooperatives prefer to sign big contracts with state enterprises than to go after small profits in the consumer market. This emerging alliance between state economic officials and leaders of cooperatives is most worrying to the authorities, afraid of losing even more of their already weakened grip on the economy. Cooperative prices are so exorbitant that 63 per cent of Muscovites never buy from them.[63]

Despite all these difficulties, the cooperative movement is managing to establish itself. In November 1988 there were 47,700 cooperatives employing 770,000 people (but only 60 per cent of these actually function – 40 per cent are mere paper formalities).[64] A situation is developing in the USSR similar to that in the other socialist countries such as Poland, Yugoslavia and Hungary: employees of the state sector with no second job are growing poorer while those of the enterprising fringe are making fortunes. Society is becoming sharply divided by wealth, with all the tensions that that entails, and without a political system capable of negotiating them. Accustomed to solving problems by prohibition and repression, the regime is finding itself at a loss as to how to handle a situation which requires regulation.

In agriculture the initial enthusiasm of the media for land leasing has given way to disillusionment: 'The rural worker has been given the right to be an independent producer. But for the moment, candidates wanting to take advantage of this right are hardly numerous.'[65] The farmer leases land from the president of the kolkhoz, and not directly from the state, and therefore remains dependent on the kolkhoz. But the real problem is elsewhere: 'Many hopes were placed in family groups. But the problem arises: where are the families? A husband, a wife and a child – is that a family?' The reforms in China are therefore not applicable to the RSFSR. Attitudes are also set against land leasing. The kolkhozian who has his land on lease is persecuted by his neighbours, who sabotage his seed and equipment, slash the tyres of his tractors, and put kerosene in his milk.[66]

We are unlikely to be able to make farmers out of thousands and thousands of people who have lost all belief in anything, who drink and have lost their natural talent. We might open hundreds of co-operative cafes, but you cannot raise from the tomb what has been destroyed over the past years [a reference to the slaughter and deportation of peasants during the enforced collectivisation between 1930 and 1933].[67]

In spite of the Decrees of September 1987, meat production in the private sector did not increase in 1988. The financial problems of kolkholzes have worsened, as the price of equipment and fertilisers have risen while that of produce has not.

Despite Gorbachevian rhetoric, the Soviet economy is continuing to follow its own course. Abalkin commented in his speech to the 19th CPSU Conference that the increase in the gross national product during the *perestroika* years has been less than the increase over the 11th 5-year Plan, during the period of 'stagnation'. According to him, nothing has yet been achieved: 'A choice had to be made: quantity or quality.' Another delegate added: 'In our attempts to break up the outdated economic mechanism, we have not sought to create anything new or more efficient, but have for the moment been satisfied to change the trappings of top level administration.' This idea that nothing has been done recurs in several speeches: 'We are limiting administrative measures from above, but we have not yet created any economic measures.'

Basically, the 19th Party Conference admitted that a new NEP was impossible. In 1921 it was enough for the Party to adopt a little self-restraint for society to regain momentum as it had not yet been destroyed. In 1987 the Party tried to do the same thing again, but without result. 'It is only now that we realise the disaster in our economy,' added a third delegate. 'Even in the worst days after the war, the shops were not so empty,' said one Muscovite.[68]

The experience of the first three years of *perestroika* sums up the whole experience of communism. Programmed to destroy, the Party finds itself completely at a loss when there is nothing left to wreck. Perfectly at ease when cracking down on unearned income and pressuring the population, it is helpless when the time comes to 'regather the stones', as the Russians say, or to rebuild the ruins.

Political reform

Every ruling Communist Party faces a major difficulty: once its absolute monopoly of power has been imposed, how does it explain the catastrophes and setbacks brought about by socialism? How can the Party be absolved of responsibility for the failure of the policies it has introduced?

Theoretical socialism postulates a homogeneous society in which Party, state and people are all one. Socialism in practice requires enemies who can be blamed for any fiasco and made public scapegoats. From the beginning, therefore, the Party had to accept the idea of social differentiation, on condition that it was wholly determined by the Party and did not represent anything real in society. Imaginary categories of enemies were immediately concocted and held up for opprobrium: English agents, lurking White Russians, the bourgeoisie, the NEPmen, kulaks and, even from the beginning, bureaucrats. Afterwards came Trotskyists, Hitler's agents, various deviationists, etc.

This fantastic menagerie may have had a certain usefulness while faith in ideology survived and while the Terror was spreading panic and demoralisation. But with de-Stalinisation, ideology suffered a crisis and communism was forced to rethink its mythology. Plausibility was now required. Foreign agents retreated into the background (to be brought forward on important occasions – even today all nationalist leaders, whether Crimean Tatars, Balts, or Armenians, are accused of being in the pay of foreigners). Instead, public antagonism was to be channelled against the bureaucrats, of whom people had daily experience.

Even this increasing moderation could not halt the decay of ideology. The failure of socialism had become so obvious, and Soviet Man so sceptical, that new sacrifices were required. *Glasnost* was the next step. The Party did not renounce its monopoly to make social differentiations but it realised that they must be made sociologically plausible. *Glasnost* served to give credibility to differentiations which remain basically arbitrary because determined by the Party. Thus the 'bureaucrats' were brought to life: their privileges, lifestyle and shady dealings were described. Other culprits – also believable from common experience – to be exposed by *glasnost* were lazy and drunken workers living off the state; greedy speculators profiting from hardship; immovable and tyrannical directors of enterprises or collective farms, ministries obsessed by their own petty interests, and so forth. Soviet theoreticians now recognise that socialist society is heterogeneous, that special interest groups exist and can conflict. The Party now permits differences of opinion (on condition that they all support socialism, differing only in the idea of how to achieve it). The regime has now completely buried its original dream of unity of state, Party and society.

An analysis of the Polish crisis, recently published in *Literaturnaya Gazeta*, gives the key to the change of attitude and to the political reform in the USSR:

The events in Poland showed to what extent it is dangerous for the Party and the government to be closely linked: when the economy weakens and political conflicts break out, society blames the Party and the system on the slightest pretext, because no one – opposition, church, trade unions – will accept the burden of responsibility.[69]

The Party has realised that even its power may be subject to wear and tear, and that it has fewer remedies for that at its disposal than a democracy. Here again is the boomerang effect: by assuming total power, the Party ends up responsible for all the nation's setbacks. As de Tocqueville said,

The government had long been suffering an illness – that common and incurable malady of every power which has undertaken to ordain all, predict all, and achieve all. It was accountable for all. And all, however divided on the nature of their grievance, heartily united in laying all blame upon it.

The Gorbachevites have realised the urgency of finding a way out of this predicament. They are camouflaging the Party's power as much as possible instead of flaunting it as in Stalin's and Brezhnev's time. This means the implication of the whole of Soviet society in the Communist fiasco. Thus 'socialist pluralism' emerges, which is a response to the crisis described in the first chapter:

The Party has in many cases supplanted state and government organisations and taken their functions upon itself. At the same time, it takes upon itself all the grievances that workers harbour against these state and government organisations, thus enabling them to take shelter behind its back, to fall into the habit of never taking decisions or feeling themselves responsible . . . the complaints of all disgruntled people fall on the Party.[70] Economic functionaries have become used to hiding behind the raikom and gorkom . . . this or that official can often be heard complaining that building projects lack cement, wood, bricks. 'We have told everyone, including the gorkom, about the situation, but it does not improve.' We would like to ask such big-mouths: 'Where is your initiative, your spirit of enterprise?'
It is time to stop passing the buck to the gorkoms when the real problem is the incompetence of functionaries in the purely economic Ministries.[72]

It is understandable that political reform should be couched in such vague terms and be advancing so slowly. The Party is trying to stage an ostensible withdrawal from society without giving up any real power ('the Party in power can never renounce its leading role of economic development . . . there is no economic, social or administrative question outside the Party's jurisdiction'[73]). The chosen solution is to create new bodies and institutions, or to reactivate those already in existence, giving them enough apparent autonomy to make them responsible in the eyes of the population: 'The Party's leading role laid down by the constitution has nothing to do with monopoly of power. To lead presupposes the distribution of power – to local Soviets, to economically autonomous enterprises, to courts, to self-management, to mass organisations.[74] But the Party makes sure that this autonomy never becomes genuine. It is reverting to its former tactics of infiltration: 'The CPSU implements its political line using those Communists occuying functions in state organs, economic organs and in all spheres of the life of society.'[75]

There is no question of really separating the Party from the state; rather a matter of making state organs a disguised arm of the Party, with more efficient agents than formerly. *Pravda* recalls Lenin's statement that Communists 'must not do everything, exhausting themselves in the process and never finding enough time: embarking on 20 projects and never finishing one; but they must control the activities of hundreds of aides'.[76] This applies chiefly to the Soviets, the 'double nature' of which Gorbachev recently stressed: 'They are both state organs and mass organisations'[77] – in other words, conveyor belts. The much-vaunted 're-valuation' threatens to be a poisoned fruit, as henceforth the Soviets will be the Party's lightning-rod:

It is disgusting that some leaders can see the queues without even trying to make the effort to do something about them. . . . All these problems, comrades, must be solved by the Soviets. And if the President of a Soviet ignores them, he is out of touch with public opinion, and it is a mistake to give him a position of responsibility . . . *perestroika* gives people real possibilities of calling to account those who do not behave according to the laws of conscience.[78]
The Soviets will take on their shoulders the main burden of state tasks and must become the active promoters of the economic, social and national policies of the Party.[79]

To avoid any drifting from the Party, the Soviets are anchored to it by the requirement to 'elect' to the leadership of the Soviet the head of the Party organisation at the same level. This does not prevent official propagandists from boasting of 'the separation of state and Party' promised by the reforms. Scepticism about the real consequences of this 'rediscovery' of the Soviets may be reinforced by the recollection that over the past 15 years 14 Decrees have been adopted to 'improve their activity'.[80]

The same institutional lightning-conductor is used at the top state level. Here, the regime does not hesitate to ape Western democracy, hoping to reap benefits both at home and abroad: at home to repair the general wearing-out of its power, and abroad to give itself social-democratic credentials for entry into the 'European Community house'. The role of the Council Ministers has thus been increased (another likely scapegoat: no doubt we shall soon see 'governments' falling in the USSR as they do in Italy). A new body has been created – the Congress of People's Deputies – with 2,500 seats of which 750 are reserved for representatives of mass organisations (Party, Komsomol, veterans' and women's associations). The Congress is responsible for electing a bicameral Supreme Soviet. The principle of multi-candidate elections has been retained, but each candidate must be registered by a regional electoral commission before acceptance. The composition of this commission has not been specified. The system has aroused fierce criticism – from the official press as well as in *samizdat* documents – rightly stressing that the Brezhnevian electoral law of 1978 was more constitutional, as it did not entail a two-stage election and respected the principle of 'one man one vote', unlike the present laws. It would be unwise to underestimate foreign policy considerations in these structural changes. Gorbachev has said that the election of the CPSU leader as head of state is desirable for 'better representation in world affairs'.[81] In order to make parliamentary exchanges plausible, the Supreme Soviet must be given some weight.

This camouflage of the Party does not only serve the defensive purpose of preventing the economic crisis from becoming a political one. Gorbachev has spoken several times of 'resuscitating the Party of Leninist foundations'. The political leadership constantly deplores the bureaucratisation of mass organisations, and their reduction to a pure formality. This criticism of bureaucracy reflects the Party's awareness that it has lost touch with the country and can no longer control and mobilise the masses. Party power is concentrated in a few specific channels: the ministries, the economic management machine, local Party committees, and mass organisations which are mostly active only on paper. Soviet society has succeeded in developing defences to many of the Party's encroachments: even the economy, as has been seen, manages to deflect them. Young people escape the Komsomol through 'informal associations' and above all, gangs. Adults take refuge in various 'nooks' – moonlighting jobs, small groups, mafias, and so forth. The ideological breakdown is total, and the grip of communism on people's minds purely negative – there is no belief, but no healthy intellectual climate can develop.

To recapture society, the CPSU must short-circuit the existing machine (one *Pravda* reader suggested the creation of a 'Komsomol within the Komsomol'[82]), and even pretend to sacrifice it. This is the origin of the various movements in support of *perestroika*, the flowering of 'informal' groups and the reactivation of mass organisation like the Komsomol, trade unions (kindly invited by the Party to defend the interests of the workers), women's movements, veterans' associations, and the revival of grassroots Communist cells in the name of 'democratisation'. There is talk of the state payng the leader of each of these cells a salary to ensure his independence from the director of the enterprise and of lightening his work load to give him more time for political activity. Reintroducing the Party into society to face the masses serves four related purposes: purging and disciplining the Party, re-rooting it in the population, creaming off the best people, and nipping potential opposition in the bud by winning its leaders over to *perestroika*. 'The people, embodied in their leaders, will penetrate political structures, air their problems, reduce alienation, and take the burden of responsibility. And in that they will save these structures.'[83]

This assault on the Party apparatus and concomitant reinforcement of Gorbachev's personal power is the second side of political *perestroika*. The outlook for the Party is more favourable here, as it has long been used to operating in this theatre. Ever since 1917 it has been waging war on the 'bureaucracy'. But even so it has been obliged to be inventive. The mafia's encroachment on the state and Party machine had never gone as far as during the long period of 'stagnation'. Never before had cadres had such uninterrupted opportunity to establish personal fiefdoms: never before had 'parallel networks' been able to flourish so widely or take such deep root. There is more than a whiff of the Chinese Cultural Revolution about *perestroika*, and this must not be underestimated:

Under Brezhnev, there began a period of duplication of power, calmly accepted by both sides. The political leadership, while proclaiming noble socialist intentions, closed its eyes to the fact that these had not been realised, and joined forces with the bureaucratic apparatus . . . at present, this formerly peaceful duplication is becoming more and more fraught with conflict . . . its liquidation in favour of the political leadership is the bridgehead of *perestroika*.[84]

The re-establishment of top Party control over the Party apparatus has so far taken various forms:

Glasnost, which enables the Centre to supervise the activities of regional satraps and to instil a salutary fear in cadres.

Purges 'The negative phenomena affecting the Party have been made possible because for a long time there has not been a single effective purge in its ranks . . . if the Party finds within itself the strength to purge its ranks of careerists, chatterboxes and ne'er-do-wells, then that could be called real *perestroika*.'[85] The purges began with the MVD. In July 1983 a political watchdog committee was set up within the Ministry charged with carrying out the purge previously prepared by Andropov. Between 1983 and 1985, at least 161,000 MVD functionaries were sacked; in 1986 12,600, in 1987 10,700. Not even top officials were spared. For A. Anikiev, President of Political Direction in the MVD, it was a question of reinforcing Party control over the Ministry.[86] Calls for the purges were resounding in the press on the eve of the 19th CPSU Conference (June 1988), but they were nevertheless postponed until later. In 1986–7 327,000 Party members were expelled.[87] Gorbachev, following in Andropov's footsteps, undertook to replace the leadership at high level. From January 1986 40 per cent of Ministers were new appointees and in 1987 40–50 per cent of Party Secretaries at Republic, regional and city level were replaced. By 1988 only 19.7 per cent of regional Party leaders were left over from the Brezhnev era: 80 per cent of Ministers were those appointed under Gorbachev.[88] 'Our first task is to restore the image of the pure and honest Communist leader.'[89]

The political leadership despatched small-scale Robespierres into the republics, charged with restoring order in local affairs, and above all with re-establishing central authority. Even so, the broom of *perestroika* is not making the clean sweep the authorities had hoped for. The press complains that in Kazakhstan and Uzbekistan family loyalties are strong enough to enable compromised officials to remain in their post. Another interesting element, most alarming to the regime, is that the population sometimes sides with convicted cadres. This was the case at Rostov-on-Don, where the Director of the Commercial Section, imprisoned for corruption, died in detention. There was a mass demonstration at his funeral. *Literaturnaya Gazeta* indignantly reported that his fellow-citizens were finding excuses for him, calling him a 'victim of the system'.[90]

This episode revealed that the parallel networks are deeply rooted in the population and that the mafias can bring people on to the streets. The purges have consequently had a destabilising effect that explains the caution of the new team and its insistence on 're-education' of cadres, even if some members do still dream of re-creating the lean and mean Party of Lenin's day.

Controls At the June 1987 CPSU Plenum, Gorbachev called for a 'unique and global system of control with full powers over the entire country' modelled on Lenin's famous 'rabkrin'. In his speech to the 19th Party Conference Gorbachev announced his proposal to appoint one of the vice-presidents to the Supreme Soviet as President of the Popular Control Committee of the USSR. In other words, the head of Popular Control will answer directly to the head of state. In these circumstances, the Committee cannot but become an instrument of Gorbachev's personal power. Nothing reveals better the Leninist spirit of the current leadership (disguised as new thinking) than its obsession with control, the idea that it is enough to institute an efficient control mechanism to supervise implementation of decisions for everything to work out as if by magic. 'It is impossible not to see that one of the causes of the serious errors of our recent past has been the weakening of the organs of control, as much in state organs and social organisations as within the Party itself.'[91] 'What creates bureaucracy? The absence of controls.'[92] As soon as these controls are put into place, the regime feels, *perestroika* will have won the day. But how do the present controls differ from previous ones which failed to avert all kinds of 'distortions' of socialism? 'The only sure way to destroy the bureaucracy is election and rotation of officials, and the immediate introduction of a system where all exercise functions of control and supervision, where all become bureaucrats temporarily so that no one can become a bureaucrat.'[93]

This is how the famous Gorbachevian 'democratisation' must be understood: it is not a progression in the idea of representation, but more an equal sharing in the policing of society from within. Under Brezhnev the authorities at the top kept watch on their subordinates without the latter being able to do the same to them. Under Gorbachev, with the aid of *glasnost*, the subordinates can now go over their bosses' heads. Control from above, inefficient because a superior can easily be got round by bribes or flattery, is much more effective when complemented by surveillance from below: it is impossible to fool your valet, as everyone knows. This clarifies *Pravda*'s comment: 'The Leninist principle of socialist control, which combines wide democratisation with the Party's leadership, must be fully implemented.'[94] In fact, this 'democratisation' indicates the determination to strengthen Communist power. *Pravda*, quoting Lenin, says: 'The more we defend a ruthlessly stronger power, the more the forms and means of control from below must be varied.'[95] 'The single guarantee of *perestroikas*'s success cannnot be other than a system of total and reliable control from bottom to top.'[96]

This notion of control is at the root of some Gorbachevian innovations in political institutions which the West wrongly interprets as progress towards democracy in the Western sense (this misunderstanding is, of course, carefully fostered by Soviet propaganda). Multi-candidate elections allow each candidate's personality to be examined under a strong light; they also check the nepotism of bureaucrats who prefer to appoint one of their own to positions of responsibility; thus it halts the mafia's expansion. But *Pravda* takes care to emphasise that these elections herald no genuine political change, or the possibility of it:

Yes, at the moment of the electoral campaign, we do not choose a political line. That was chosen long ago by the Soviet people; before placing his ballot in the box, the Soviet citizen asks about the candidate: 'What kind of a man is he? Will he be able to carry out the will of the electorate, to implement the policies of the Party and state?'[97]

The limits on terms in office (maximum two terms of five years each) serve the same purpose. 'Rotating the cadres' obviously prevents officials from establishing fiefdoms and creating networks of dependents. The election of Party committee leaders to the leadership of corresponding Soviets is explained by N. Nazarbaiev, President of the Council of Ministers for Kazakhstan, in these terms: 'From now on the Party Committee will be under dual control: that of Communists and that of deputies. I will say bluntly that I do not envy the Party functionaries.'[98]

The elections of 26 March 1989 were the culmination of Gorbachev's battle with the Communist machinery – as radical a purge as Stalin's, and carried out to Western accolades. In constituencies with more than one candidate, a 'bureaucrat' stood against one or more 'perestroikists'. Obviously, the population was not going to forgo the chance to settle scores with the hated 'bureaucrats'.

These elections, rather than representing a 'triumph of democracy' as the Western media euphorically declared, were a cynical exploitation by the Gorbachevites of the Soviet people's desire to be rid of their oppressors. They had, however, the merit of revealing the degree of Party unpopularity.

What might have happened had the elections been truly democratic – if the Soviets could have chosen between genuine political alternatives, instead of having to make do with replacing the Brezhnevite mafia with Gorbachev's young lions? The situation in the Baltic states, where the Popular Fronts have set real political stakes, the Yeltsin episode and other turns taken by the electoral campaign have shown that the Soviet population is pressing home the smallest advantage and that in a free election the CPSU would suffer an appalling return.

A new distribution of power within the Party The Party Secretariat is delegating some of its functions to the six Central Committee commissions created in 1988 (in the areas of cadres, ideology, economic and social policy, agriculture, and law). This reorganisation can only strengthen Gorbachev's position. He will now have less to fear from a too-powerful Secretariat (always a danger to the First Secretary) and will proceed to centralise these new organs.

The 'socialist rule of law'
The need to control the Party apparatus has brought the Soviet authorities to the idea of a 'socialist rule of law'. The political leadership realised that it was impossible to supervise – and make itself respected by – local authorities if the regional judiciary and KGB were entirely under the thumb of local bigwigs. 'During the period of stagnation, the regional judicial organs often transformed themselves into organs of personal protection for local officials.'[99] 'An immediate end must be brought to a situation in which the local organs of justice find themselves outside Party control', said *Pravda*, referring to Bashkiria;[100] 'Party', here, of course, means the Central Party. The new Chief Prosecutor of the USSR, A. Sukharev, declared in an interview: 'The Public Prosecutor's Department had become an appendage of the bureaucratic system of command; its centralised and independent essence had been lost . . . many prosecutors shrugged their shoulders at local abuses; sometimes they covered up arbitrariness and illegality and became accomplices.'[102] It is noteworthy that in the Chief Prosecutor's mind, 'centralised' is coupled with 'independent': this is far from Montesquieu's idea of the separation of powers. The Centre simply decided that it was preferable to curb the power of local authority power over the judiciary.

The press and the intelligentsia have taken advantage of this opportunity to criticise judicial practice by denouncing the aberrations of the system, the absence of legal tradition ('we need to return to the ABC of law')[102] and of respect for the law. The Public Prosecutor's Department is currently responsible for criminal investigation; it is also responsible for ensuring that the law is upheld in tribunals and elsewhere. If an innocent person is wrongly accused, it is the Prosecutor (in charge of the investigation) who appeals against the verdict. The abuses arising out of this system may be imagined, more so as the Defence has no access to the case file before the investigation is completed. The press reported a dramatic illustration of this 'judicial illiteracy'. For 14 years a 'ripper' had stalked the Vitebsk region, killing several young girls each year. Fourteen people were falsely accused of these murders (which sometimes carried the death penalty) before the police arrested the real culprit. Here again, the Soviet mania for norms and percentages caused mayhem: the police had to bring in 'culprits' – whether guilty or not – to keep the statistics favourable. Every kind of pressure (including torture) was applied to obtain confessions.

Judges are elected by the corresponding Soviets for a term of five years (Moscow court judges are elected by the Moscow Soviet, for example, while RSFSR Supreme Court Judges are elected by the RSFSR Supreme Soviet, and so forth). In these circumstances, the judges have no chance of asserting their independence, as local authorities have a thousand ways of settling scores with uncooperative judges – the threat of being deprived of a flat can make the boldest think twice. It may be that some of these abuses will be stopped by the reforms currently envisaged. There has been talk of turning criminal investigation over to a special body answering to the Ministry of the Interior, of increasing the use of juries, of extending the powers of defence lawyers, of having judges elected by high level committees. All this would indeed be an improvement on the present situation (though the last project now appears to have been abandoned). But even so, would the USSR really develop into a state of law? Since 1987 Soviet citizens have had the right to take state and Party functionaries, but not the KGB, to court.[103] Equality before the law was not mentioned in the judicial resolution passed at the time of the 19th CPSU Conference. A Party member cannot be brought to trial unless he is first expelled from the Party, that is unless his superiors decide to sacrifice him.

Even supposing that local judges gain a measure of independence, what guarantee is there that it will be the same at the top, given the Party's 'leading role'? *Literaturnaya Gazeta* recently wondered 'how to understand from a juridical viewpoint the formula "the Party is the kernel of the political system of Soviet society" '.[104] And indeed the entire problem lies here. The USSR has always equated legality with Party leadership. There is no difference between the executive and the legislative. In the USSR, any law – including Articles of the Constitution – can be nullified by an Executive Decree. Article 6, on the leading role of the Party, cancels out all other Articles, reducing them to mere legal ornaments. To curry favour with Western democracies, to respond to the need for reforms formulated by many intellectuals the Soviets have decided to 'revitalise' their legislative organs. But as long as the principle of representation is not admitted, the legislative bodies are condemned to remain extensions of the Party, true law to disappear beneath 'rulings', and the 'socialist rule of law' to remain an oxymoron. The same can be said about 'judicial reform' as about 'demoncratisation': the Party pretends to be taking action to meet some need in society while in fact introducing measures to reinforce centralisation and political direction, to recommunise society in depth, and to enshrine in law its own arbitrary rule. No wonder the ex-KGB chief, Chebrikov, was made head of the commission for law reform.

According to Grigoriantz, Editor-in-Chief of *Glasnost*, the legislative changes are the most dangerous in the USSR today: 'the only serious and substantial reforms':

The law on assemblies, demonstrations and meetings (adopted in October 1988) has plainly abolished the freedom of assembly which was beginning to be born in the USSR . . . the law on special forces (adopted in October 1988) has abolished the inviolability of domicile guaranteed by the Constitution . . . the law, by placing Party and Soviet power and – on the federal level – Party and legislative power in the same hands, concentrates personal power in a way unprecedented for 70 years, and with Constitutional support . . . the country is moving towards a state of law in which peacetime laws will be more severe than wartime ones.'[105]

The Decree of December 1988 outlawing publishing cooperatives makes a mockery of the Constitutional guarantee of freedom of expression.

It is a pity that Western 'Gorbomaniacs' have neglected to examine closely the legislative changes adopted in the USSR since 1985. Law is the only area in which the regime cannot afford to lie outright. The written laws speak to those who will listen, and what they say bears devastating witness to the nature of the leadership in power. The most repressive measures were voted through in the autumn of 1988, after the elimination of the so-called 'conservatives'. 'Reform' is being used as a pretext to strengthen Gorbachev's personal power, which has become so extensive as to worry Sakharov. The degree of Western misunderstanding of the Soviets and the naivety of those who see Gorbachev as a convert to social-democracy can be seen from the '*perestroikist*' weekly *Moscow News*, which writes unblushingly that

The leadership personified by Mikhal Gorbachev is the universally-recognised guarantee of *perestroika*'s success, and must be reinforced at judicial level. At the present hour, everyone is aware of the insufficient power of the top authorities, which explains the difficulties Gorbachev is encountering in the implementation of his policies.[106]

The current state of ideology
References to ideological disaffection in the population are on the increase. The press ascribes this disenchantment to the revelations of *glasnost*. One *Pravda* reader complains: 'The idea of socialism has been somehow discredited in the wake of *glasnost* and stringent criticism. . . . My faith has been shaken.'[107] Party leaders are having a hard time of it: 'It has become difficult to work with people at this time. There is a tendency to exaggerate the shortcomings, and we are more and more often obliged to explain the advantages of socialism.'[108] Certain details stand out, such as the current isolation of activist schoolchildren, considered bootlickers by their fellow

pupils.[109]

In fact, the ideological crisis did not begin with *glasnost*. Quite the contrary: *glasnost* was an attempt to stop the breakdown, with the Party dissociating itself from its own past, even taking the initiative in criticism in order to disarm potential adversaries and at the same time promote the current line. The accumulated crimes of 70 years were a threatening enough collection of time bombs to set Party ideologists trying to defuse them one by one. Considering the difficulty of the task, it is understandable that Soviet theoreticians should be rapidly altering the ideological blueprint.

Under Brezhnev it was simpler: then, there was a line that could not be crossed, and that was that. Today the ideological architects proceed differently. They have built a succession of walls which may be broached; only at the very centre is there still an impregnable fortress containing the mausoleum of Leninism. Successive layers of bandages are being applied to the mummy itself. Gorbachev's desire to create a new Party for himself impelled him to re-launch de-Stalinisation, facing its side-effects with more sang-froid than Khrushchev had shown. Nevertheless, the potentially explosive nature of *glasnost* made the job of defusing extremely delicate, as the revelations called into question the regime's very legitimacy.

Various lines of defence were accordingly drawn. The first and most prominent was the theme of the discontinuity between Lenin and Stalin, contrasting the humane and democratic Lenin with the tyrannical and insane Stalin. This main line has a number of branches, some of which have been taken from American 'new look' Sovietologists: Stalinism was not an inevitable development. Bukharin (Lenin's comrade-in-arms, author of the famous 1936 Soviet Constitution and victim of Stalin's purges) had represented the viable alternative of 'socialism with a human face'. The Bolsheviks had many martyrs, brave Communists like Kirov, who kept this tradition of democratic communism alive throughout the grim era of Stalin. This theme is important, as it creates the idea of historical continuity between those 'pure' Communists and the current *perestroikists*, thus giving legitimacy to the latter.

Pravda launched a violent attack on the historian Y. Afanassiev, who had defended the idea that socialism had gone completely wrong and must be rebuilt from A to Z. For *Pravda*, the essential thing is to correct the 'distortions of socialism' caused by Stalinist practices.[110] In both cases, historical materialism sustained a heavy blow. If there was a 'Leninist alternative' to Stalin, as Afanassiev maintained, what had become of the determinism inherent in the Marxist vision? Nevertheless, Afanassiev is no less orthodox than his detractors in *Pravda*. The Soviets now have a choice of several ideological lines: they may continue to believe that there was some good in Stalinism, despite the 'errors' blamed on Stalin's psychopathic personality (and on his immediate entourage, notably Jews such as Kaganovitch); or they may dismiss the whole Stalinist period with the idea that Stalin betrayed Lenin's ideals and that the priority now is to exert new effort to pull the chariot of socialism out of the ditch in which it is stuck. The Party is taking no sides, having cast itself in the role of arbiter and mediator, a calming force amid excessive passions. Official propaganda flirts with the fundamentalist 'conservatives' who consider Marxism as a harmful Western import, part of the great global conspiracy against the Russian people, with the 'liberal' Westernisers who dream of 'normal' existence, and with the hardcore Marxists, numerous among Gorbachev's advisers.

These last maintain another version of history, which does not necessarily contradict Afanassiev's. They say that communism, the ideal system for mankind, had the bad luck to be adopted first by the backward Russian people and has therefore become tainted with the Tzarist heritage. 'The cult of personality was not imposed solely from above. Unfortunately it reflected the phenomenon of the masses' level of political culture.'[111] This version has the advantage of involving the people in the Party's crimes (which helps to avert any calling to account); and it is completely in keeping with the current ideological spirit of *perestroika* which essentially seeks to implicate the people in the communist fiasco ('it is not the system that is responsible, but ourselves'[112]), and then to dissociate the Party from the result of its policies. Ever since it first championed *perestroika*, the Party would have us believe, it has been deploying all its resources to introduce change. It is not to blame if society – apathetic, parasitic and corrupt – does not respond to its reforms. The Party holds itself out as the sole bastion of civic spirit, public morality, reason and tolerance in a society riven by the demons of anti-Semitism, nationalist passions, banditry and sloth. To oppose *perestroika* is therefore 'to proclaim publicly that one is in favour of corruption, opposed to social equality, etc.'.[113] Who could resist such virtuous blackmail? And yet, human nature being perverse, 'The assassins of *perestroika* are among us'[114], says Yevtushenko, always quick to discern which way the wind is blowing.

We are today in the midst of a revolution, and it is most important to spot and identify the enemy. In 1917 the enemy was obvious, he was on the other side of the barricades. And where is he today? In the bureaucracy? Certainly. In the immovable functionary? Without doubt . . . but the main enemy of *perestroika* lurks deep inside each one of us.[115]

This line is doubly pernicious: it has aggravated the demoralisation of the society, increased intellectual confusion (this can be seen especially in Poland, where it has been applied with particular Machiavellianism. The Polish referendum on reform aimed to lay the blame for the lack of change on the people, with the Party assuming the role of far-sighted guardian and initiator of the public good); and above all it has worked in the West, where most political leaders sympathise with Gorbachev in his struggle with the deplorable 'human factor'. The media have begun to discuss the writings of American historian and Russian specialist, Richard Pipes, which emphasise the continuity between the Soviet past and present, i.e. between tzarism and Bolshevism. This serves a twofold purpose: first, to absolve the Party of its 'errors' by laying all blame on the tzarist past and the heritage of serfdom; secondly, to fan Russian nationalism covertly to the advantage of official propaganda, by letting the Russians see that the West considers them as pariahs among the civilised nations.

Communism has always exploited national inferiority complexes and today *perestroika*, which discloses the distance separating peoples under communism from those in the democratic societies, plays this to the hilt. The Party sells itself to the West, and to Westernised intellectuals at home, as the only force for enlightenment in the USSR. For the benefit of ordinary Soviet citizens, it concentrates on its role in world affairs and its leadership in international relations. In this it manipulates the ambivalence characteristic of 'Soviet man'. On the one hand, he is proud to see his rulers deceiving the West and on the other, profoundly discouraged to see the rest of the world won over by totalitarianism. Domestic propaganda takes pains to point out to the captive peoples that there will be no help from the outside world, that the world has adopted the slogans of *glasnost* and *perestroika* (i.e. the CPSU line), that Gorbachev has the approval of the world, in fact is more popular than Reagan was in West Germany. The most effusive eulogies to Gorbachev are those quoted from foreigners. Thus, French Sovietologist, Lilly Marcou, declares in *Moscow News*: 'Gorbachev is the pioneer of a new order that will show the value of everything positive that socialism has accumulated over the last 70 years.'[116] Jaruzelski is not to be outdone, either: 'It sometimes happens that the personality of a leader, his activity and his resolute character inspire millions of people. Permit me to include you among those leaders.'[117]

The Khrushchevian bluster on the imminent economic successes of socialism is no longer to be heard. The media recognise, implicitly or explicitly, that socialism may be inferior to capitalism in respect of economic efficiency and standards of living. The ideologists' one unshakeable line is the moral superiority of socialism, which they expound in pathos-laden terms: 'The social revolution is the one way to the temple of spiritual purification for society and humanism.'[118] The ambiguity of the term 'socialism' is put to good use. Attempts are made to associate Lenin with European Social Democracy, and to disguise the specifics of Leninism. This deliberate confusion serves foreign policy aims, but also gives a badly-needed polish to the tarnished image of socialism. The bottom line is that socialism is intrinsically better, never mind the evidence. Whenever people can, they choose socialism.

The ideological canon has lost some of its rigidity. More than one view of history is permitted, but on one condition: that they all adopt the frame of reference handed down from above (which happens to be a false one). Those who refuse, who do not accept the premiss of the superiority of socialism, are accused of 'negativism'. They are treated as 'extremists' fuelled by a spirit of 'confrontation' (an extremely pejorative term in Gorbachevian sovspeak, meaning rejection of communism and opposite of 'realism', which translates as 'acceptance of communism'). They are urged to move to 'constructive' criticism, i.e. to recognise the regime's legitimacy, and to show some 'impartiality', in other words, to look on the bright side of socialism instead of focusing on 'the errors and crimes'.

In canvassing for propaganda lines and flirting with the social democracies, Soviet ideologists are playing on all Western themes compatible with the Leninist spirit of destruction, swallowing, digesting and regurgitating them in the USSR, the West and the Third World, where they are spread with the help of the powerful communist propaganda machine. Some of these themes are worth examining:

• The nuclear threat: happily the USSR has realised this danger and is now the spokesman of mankind for the denuclearisation of our planet. In exploiting the fear of a nuclear apocalypse, the USSR has rediscovered its messianic mission and finds itself once again the self-appointed apostle of humanity's salvation.
• The ecological peril: here again, the socialist countries have the right and duty to be in the vanguard, as they have not been corrupted by the profit ethic, and for them, the interest of all comes before that of a few selfish groups.
• Aid to poor countries: once more the USSR is demonstrating disinterested generosity in urging Third World nations to default on their debts.
• The leading role of intellectuals: in the USSR, intellectuals enjoy a privileged position. Gorbachev takes the advice of scientists, while the West consigns them to the fringe.

These themes are by no means new, but they have come to the forefront now that class struggle has been shelved. Anything, nihilistic, hostile to civilisation, false or stupid from the West is eagerly snapped up and recycled by the Soviets for use at home and abroad. When it is not harping on Leninist slogans, Gorbachevian discourse is an anthology of distressing platitudes, a terrifying reflection of the intellectual bankruptcy of our time. Its success in the Western media is doubtless due to this.

Thus, current Soviet propaganda is innovative in that it is borrowing more from abroad and brushing up its own terminology. Theoretical writings show that Soviet authors have perfected the art of making a scenic tour of modern concepts signalling 'new thinking', only to return to the starting point – the most primitive Brezhnevian ideology stereotype.

The following is an example of this pattern:

We have no classes or social groups . . . with radically or profoundly divergent interests. What we have, on the other hand, are divergences and contradictions, certainly important, but temporary, latent conflicts between innovators and conservatives, between the supporters and the hidden adversaries of *perestroika*. Given the provisional nature of these divergences (which will disappear with *perestroika*, once it is realised) the question of concurrent political parties cannot arise.[119]

This extract shows a number of the favourite techniques of the new propaganda: for example, the notion of 'conservatives vs. innovators' (supposedly to 'Left vs. Right') has been borrowed from the West. It is being built over Soviet reality like a stage set, raising a false debate and disguising what goes on behind the scenes – the power struggle, the outcome of which is predetermined, as *perestroika* is bound to take the upper hand. The political pattern (Left vs. Right), borrowed from the West, is giving a democratic veneer, and thus legitimacy, to the Party in its age-old struggle with various deviations. Another example of false evolution, hiding the reinforcement of Leninism, is the ostensible renunciation of 'class values' in the name of higher human values. As *Pravda* says: 'Today there cannot be any hope of success in the class struggle unless we arm ourselves with slogans appealing to the interests of all humanity.'[120]

The ideological policy of the Gorbachev team is an image of *perestroika* itself. Bogus concessions are advertised, roads leading nowhere are opened, fierce controversy whipped up over non-existent issues. All this serves to distract attention from the question of power and its nature, to spread intellectual confusion and to sow division in potential opposition. In such division the regime seeks its salvation, more than in any of the dubious 'reforms'.

NOTES

1. V. Pozner in *Sovietskaya Kultura*, 16 December 1986.
2. *LG*, 29 July 1987.
3. *Pravda*, 8 January 1988.
4. *Works*, vol. 36, p. 149.
5. *LG*, 8 October 1987.
6. M. Gorbachev, Speech of 19 February 1987.
7. XIXth CPSU Conference.
8. *Pravda*, 5 August 1988.
9. *Liberation*, 19 January 1989.
10. 13 February 1987.
11. *RLRB*, 1 December 1987.
12. Murmansk speech, 1 October 1987.
13. *RLRB*, 19 and 26 August 1987.
14. *Strana y Mir*, no. 5, 1987, pp. 66–73; *Possey*, no. 4, 1988.
15. 13 March 1987.
16. *LG*, 3 December 1986.
17. *Pravda*, 24 May 1987.
18. 17 August 1986.
19. *LG*, 5 August 1987.
20. *LG*, 15 June 1988.
21. M. Gorbachev, Speech to the Plenum, 29 July 1988.
22. *RLRB*, 18 March 1987.
23. *RLRB*, 19 August 1987.
24. *RLRB*, 18 March 1987.

25. *LG*, 21 September 1988.
26. *Moscow News*, 11 September 1988.
27. *Moscow News*, 22 May 1988.
28. *RLRB*, 25 May 1988.
29. *LG*, 6 April 1988.
30. No. 12.
31. *Pravda*, 12 September 1987 and 15 October 1987.
32. *Moscow News*, 19 June 1988.
33. XIXth CPSU Conference.
34. *Pravda*, 8 July 1988.
35. USSR News Brief, no. 12, 1986.
36. *Morskoy Sbornik*, no. 8, 1987, pp. 10–11,
37. *Moscow News*, 10 April 1988.
38. System by which a set task is turned over to a self-managing group in exchange for a sum of money.
39. *Moscow News*, 17 April 1988.
40. *RLRB*, 28 October 1987.
41. XIXth CPSU Conference.
42. *Pravda*, 7 July 1988.
43. *Pravda*, 31 August 1988.
44. XIXth CPSU Conference.
45. M. Gorbachev, Speech to the XIXth CPSU Conference.
46. XIXth CPSU Conference.
47. *Moscow News*, 10 April 1988.
48. XIXth CPSU Conference.
49. *Pravda*, 25 April 1988.
50. *Communist of the Armed Forces*, no. 18, September 1988, p. 24; no. 22, November 1988, p. 22.
51. *Pravda*, 16 August 1988.
52. 3 August 1987.
53. *Pravda*, 3 September 1988.
54. *LG*, 28 September 1988.
55. *LG*, 20 July 1988 and Moscow News, 18 September 1988.
56. *Pravda*, 13 October 1987 and 1 December 1987.
57. *RLRB*, 12 and 26 October 1988.
58. E. Primakov in *Pravda*, 20 March 1988.
59. *Pravda*, 18 May 1988.
60. *LG*, 9 March 1988.
61. *Pravda*, 1 December 1987.
62. *LG*, 24 August 1988.
63. *LG*, 11 January 1989.
64. *Moscow News*, 20 November 1988.
65. *LG*, 24 August 1988.
66. *Pravda*, 3 and 4 July 1988.
67. *LG*, 27 July 1988.
68. *Pensée Russe*, 30 September 1988.
69. 12 October 1988.
70. XIXth CPSU Conference.
71. *Pravda*, 31 May 1988.

72. *Pravda*, 10 June 1988.
73. *Pravda*, 20 July 1988.
74. *LG*, 30 March 1988.
75. M. Gorbachev, Speech to XIXth CPSU Conference.
76. *Pravda*, 27 July 1988.
77. Speech, 29 November 1988.
78. M. Gorbachev, Speech to the Plenum, 29 July 1988.
79. M. Gorbachev, Speech to the Supreme Soviet, 1 October 1988.
80. *Communist of the Armed Forces*, no. 20, October 1988, p. 79.
81. XIXth CPSU Conference.
82. 12 October 1987.
83. A. Prokhanov in *LG*, 20 July 1988.
84. *Moscow News*, 5 June 1988.
85. *Pravda*, 8 May 1988.
86. *RLRB*, 27 April 1987, 13 April 1988, 3 August 1988.
87. *Communist of the Armed Forces*, no. 24, December 1988, p. 39.
88. *RLRB*, 29 January 1986, 21 October 1987 and 15 June 1988.
89. M. Gorbachev, Speech to the Plenum, January 1987.
90. 7 January 1987.
91. *Pravda*, 15 July 1987.
92. *Pravda*, 10 February 1988.
93. *Pravda*, 24 August 1987.
94. *Pravda*, 24 September 1987.
95. *Pravda*, 26 February 1988.
96. *Pravda*, 13 May 1988.
97. *Pravda*, 8 May 1987 and 28 May 1987.
98. *Pravda*, 9 July 1988.
99. *Moscow News*, 20 March 1988.
100. *Pravda*, 6 July 1987.
101. *LG*, 31 August 1988.
102. *LG*, 27 January 1988.
103. *RLRB*, 17 August 1988.
104. *LG*, 8 June 1988.
105. *Pensée Russe*, 18 November 1988.
106. 30 October 1988.
107. *Pravda*, 18 January 1988.
108. *LG*, 16 December 1987.
109. *Pravada*, 23 September 1987.
110. *Pravda*, 26 and 31 July 1988.
111. F. Burlatsky in *Pravda*, 18 July 1987.
112. *LG*, 28 October 1987.
113. E. Yakovlev, quoted in *RLRB*, 1 December 1987.
114. *LG*, 11 May 1988.
115. XIXth CPSU Conference.
116. 23 October 1988.
117. *Pravda*, 12 July 1988.
118. *LG*, 12 October 1988.
119. B. Kurachvili in *Moscow News*, 6 March 1988.
120. *Pravda*, 13 April 1988.

4.   Gorbachev and religion

For some time now the Soviet authorities have appeared to be introducing a note of *perestroika* into their longstanding hostility to religion. In 1987–8 the Communist Party conducted numerous goodwill overtures, a such as returning to the Orthodox Church monasteries and chapels long ago requisitioned by the state. One of these, the St Daniel Monastery, has been assigned by the regime to the Moscow Patriarchate as an administration centre, to house its most important section (the Sector for Foreign Relations, funnily enough). In Moscow, the authorities are no longer recording the passport numbers of couples marrying in church or baptising their children.

There is even talk of revising the legislation pertaining to religion – making parishes into legal entities, for example. The media have been frowning on the tangle of red tape which hampers the registering of religious congregations, and even giving a platform to religious dignitaries. Archbishop Pitirim has been on Soviet television pleading the cause of *glasnost* and *perestroika*. The monthly review *Kommunist* has suggested that religious believers might conceivably make decent citizens. A kosher restaurant has opened in Moscow. To cap it all, Gorbachev recently received – at the Kremlin, with great ceremony – Patriarch Pimen, together with his chief bishops.

Since April 1987 there has been a veritable pilgrimage to Moscow of assorted foreign religious celebrities – Mother Teresa, Cardinal Sin of the Philippines, the Dalai Lama, various French bishops, even a delegation from the World Islamic Congress.[1]

All this has been more than enough to set the Western medias talking about a 'historic compromise' between the Communist regime and Soviet believers, and marvelling once again at Gorbachev's spirit of innovation. In these circumstances, it is worth examining more closely the actual religious policies of the Soviet Union in this era of *glasnost*, first to avoid hasty and ill-informed judgements, but more importantly because these policies are typical of Gorbachev's overall strategy and tactics.

What is the Orthodox Church, in the eyes of the Party ideologists? A recent *Pravda* article says it clearly:

The social position of the Orthodox Church has altered considerably over the period of its operation in our society. Originally it was a feudal church, a state institution of the Russian empire, defending the oppressors' interests and fuelled by exploitation of the masses. It has evolved into a voluntary association of citizens with religious beliefs, independent of the state, financed by its members. Its sphere of influence and its field of activity have narrowed. Unlike the old Orthodox Church of the first years of the revolution, which openly defended anti-socialist positions and refused to accept the power of the people, the modern Church recognises the socialist system. It supports the domestic and foreign policy of the Soviet state. . . . The very fact of this fundamental change, without precedent in the history of religion, bears eloquent witness to the radical and profound nature of socialist transformation, which has left its imprint even on an institution as conservative as the Church. Moreover, it constitutes a refutation of the basic theological premise of the divine foundation of the Orthodox Church.[2]

This last sentence is particularly revealing. The Orthodox Church is not now simply required to back the regime in its pursuit of various foreign and domestic goals: it must be on display, docile and sycophantic, as a living vindication of Marxist 'historical materialism'. If God has permitted an atheist state to bring His own church to heel, it must follow that He does not exist. The spectacular favours granted to the Orthodox Church, in exchange for its public engagements in the cause of *perestroika* and (Western) disarmament, are all to this end. They are simply another aspect of the Gorbachev regime's campaign against religion – the Gorbachev who announced in Tashkent in 1986 that 'We must fight a determined and ruthless battle against religion, intensifying atheist propaganda.'

The televised exhibition of Patriarch Pimen assuring viewers in excellent sovspeak that 'The Orthodox Church's flock, all believers and non-believing citizens, welcome with all their heart the process of spiritual, social and economic renewal of Soviet society, which has become irreversible: the process of *perestroika*, democratisation and *glasnost*,'[3] the sight of Metropolitans bedecked with Soviet medals such as the Order of the Red Flag and the Order of Friendship between Peoples, are far more effective ways to disillusion believers than hundreds of overtly 'atheist' conferences exposing priests' duplicity and demonstrating religion to be 'in the pay of imperialism and reaction'. Just why has the author Aitmatov, in his latest novel *The Scaffold*, introduced the figure of Christ simply to have him spout pure *Pravda* slogans? And Gorbachev has shown himself to have inherited Stalin's black humour in his unblushing speech to Orthodox bishops: 'The Leninist decreee [of separation of Church and state] opened the possibility for the Church of realising its activity without any outside interference. . . . The spirit of liberation of the great October Revolution touched all the religious organisations of our multi-national state.' The recollection that during the 1920s believers and priests were hunted down, imprisoned and shot by the thousand shows Gorbachev's talent for the apt formula. It is interesting to imagine the effect on Orthodox believers of Patriarch Pimen's response: 'We pride ourselves on the restoration of Leninist principles in religious policy, and we believe that this will strengthen the unity of our people and the prestige of our homeland.'

Consequently, it is not at all advisable to judge the Soviet regime's current policies toward religious believers on the basis of its gestures made to the officially-tolerated churches, the leaders of which are in effect cassocked CPSU spokesmen. Much more significant are the Party's attitudes to the various unofficial, non-registered sects, as well as to the dissidents within the official churches; the tasks that have been assigned to Party propagandists; and particularly the analyses of Party ideologists.

As an example of the latter, the latest discovery of Gorbachev's theoreticians is that:

Religious belief does not only survive because of the legacy of the past, but also because of the limitations – the incomplete development – of our society. Clearly, it cannot be denied that the process of social distortions of all kinds has greatly contributed to the conservation of religiosity in the nation.[4]

This is a rather daring application of classic Marxism to contemporary Soviet society. Religious belief – the 'opium of the people' – persists because the population still needs the promise of a better world to compensate for the present one. The 'social causes' of religion, far from having disappeared, are being more than ever felt. In these circumstances, what worries the theoreticians is that

when considering the moral problems of modern society and confronting the phenomena of spiritual emptiness, corruption and criminality, some people – those lacking strength of principle – are taking pains to show that formerly the Church took a stand against such evils, and they call for a return to religious morality. . . . This state of mind is especially evident now, on the eve of the millennium of Russia's conversion to Christianity, and must be tackled from a Marxist–Leninist standpoint, without idealisation or slander. Moreover, it must be demonstrated that it is not religion that has given people the norms of common humanity. These were developed by the masses in the course of their secular struggle against the inhumanity and amoralism of the exploiters' system.[5]

This extract confronts an alarming attitude spreading throughout the USSR, the best evidence of which is in a novel by the peasant writer Astafiev,[6] *The Blind Fisherman*, published in 1986:

What has become of us? Who hurled us into this abyss of evil and calamity? What for? Who killed the light of Good in our souls? Who blew out the candle of our conscience and tossed it into this black pit that we stumble through, seeking the firm ground of the lowest depths and the glimmer of future hope? What good is a beacon leading into the flames of Hell? Our souls once shone with the light the saints struck to save us from wandering blind in the forest, lashing out at trees and our fellow men, clawing each others' eyes, breaking the bones of those nearest us. Why did they take it all away and give us nothing in return but unbelief? Who will hear our prayers? Whose forgiveness can we beg?

In the face of this sort of thing, there can surely be no question of relaxing ideological vigilance with regard to the Orthodox Church, even if completely tamed.

'The Church's political loyalty and its addressing of crucial contemporary problems could lead to a certain strengthening of its ideological position in society. For this reason an intensification of atheist propaganda among all sections of the population, particularly the young, is necessary.'[7] 'In the present conditions, one of the most urgent tasks for atheist propaganda is to oppose principles of socialist morality to religious moral precepts.'[8]

This clear-eyed assessment of the situation accounts for the instructions to propagandists to use 'tact' and 'sensitivity' in inculcating atheism in the population; and it explains *Literaturnaya Gazeta*'s criticising 'the same endless anti-religious demagogy, going on *ad nauseam*'.[9] The army is widely perceived as the best practitioner of Communist indoctrination. As *Communist of the Armed Forces*, the ideological review of the military, says, 'There are still many officers and political functionaries . . . who consider religion as an adversary which has been definitively vanquished, representing no further danger.'[10] Vigilance is always necessary:

Officers, propagandists and Party and Komsomol activitists all carry anti-religious propaganda not only within the units but to the local population, in workers' collectives where the members are in frequent contact with troops. . . . There are believers among these people, who in the course of their regular contact with troops even try to convert them to their views. This fact must not be overlooked.[11]

Sad to say, here as elsewhere present performance leaves something to be desired.

Unhappily, not everyone is maintaining sufficient energy, persistence and patience in the re-education of believers among the military . . . some activists avoid the task altogether because they simply have no idea what to do about a soldier who has religious inclinations; they are completely ignorant of the elementary roots of his beliefs.[12] Propagandists of atheism ought not to forget that today they are no longer dealing with illiterate believers as in the past, but with people who for the most part have a secondary education.[13]

A more 'differentiated approach' is recommended for atheist propaganda:

It is important to define the character and particularities of the different persuasions. . . . For example, the tenets of Islam are often associated with nationalist tendencies in the minds of Moslem believers. The Baptists follow evangelical teaching. Most of the Orthodox are bound to their religion above all because of its traditional and ritualistic aspect. . . . If a propagandist speaks to people without knowing what he is dealing with, he could find himself in an absurd situation, for example criticising Christianity to Moslems, or denouncing the cult of ikons to Baptists.[14]

Above all, plans must be made to train specialist propagandists to refute Islam, given 'the demographic situation' in the country. Everything remains to be done: 'We cannot yet say that we have succeeded in formulating effective propaganda among the followers of Islam. It is a very serious problem.'[15] A final piece of advice in military writings is to stop any barrack-room bullying which 'drives the soldier or sailor to seek the support of supernatural forces', and especially to fill any spare time with 'interesting sporting activities, film shows, etc.' so that 'no one will feel the need to use free time to go to church, to draw apart in order "to turn to God".'[16]

There are none the less some new elements in Gorbachev's religious policy. Although it remains Leninist, it is precisely these Leninist considerations which have forced a revision of previous positions and tactical modifications (the long-term strategy is unchanged). By a 'creative' Leninist analysis, i.e. applying the classic Leninist categories to new circumstances, the Party realised that its religious policies had had boomerang effects similar to those described earlier. The society at large learnt to protect itself against the encroachments of the Party and to set up its own channels. The official Orthodox Church went the same way as the Komsomol, becoming bureaucratised and losing its grip on the population. Disbelief in God began to extend to disbelief in communism, which was highly undesirable. This analysis, and the remedies proposed, are interesting because they are a sort of distillation of Gorbachevism and the 'new thinking'.

An astonishing text has recently appeared in the West which contains the key to the present strategy with regard to religion. The transcript of a speech delivered to the Party's top training academy by K. Khartchev, leader at the time of the Council for Religious Affairs, it has all the frankness of early Bolshevism combined with a Leninist cynicism that is openly, almost innocently, avowed:

We, the Party, have fallen into the trap of our own anticlerical policy of prohibition and harassment, we have cut off the priest from his parishioners, but believers have not in the meantime increased their faith in the authorities; on the contrary the Party and the state are losing more and more control over believers. We have into the bargain brought about the phenomenon of indifferent believers: that is, people who perform the rites but to whom nothing matters, especially communism. What is more useful to the Party, someone indifferent or a sincere believer? It is more difficult to govern those who are indifferent . . . we must ask ourselves if someone who believes in God and in communism is not more useful to the Party than someone who believes in nothing. We must choose the lesser of two evils. According to Lenin, the Party must control all aspects of citizens' lives, and as there is no way of getting rid of believers, and history has shown that religion is here to stay, the Party must simply ensure that the sincere believer also believes in communism. And so we have a task before us: to educate a new type of priest. The choice and appointment of priests is a matter for the Party. . . . It is in the ranks of the priests and bishops of the Orthodox Church that we have had our greatest successes in controlling religion and stifling its initiative. At first we were congratulating ourselves, but this policy is now threatening to have unforeseen consequences. . . . We should be worrying about the strengthening of the other persuasions – the Catholics who are still afloat, and the sects that are thriving . . . and Catholics, protestants, evangelists, adventists and others have centres to which Soviet power has no access, and that is why their growing membership is fraught with unpredictable consequences. . . . Today our task is real control of the Church by the Party.

Khartchev further criticises the brutal anti-religious campaigns and the physical destruction of churches, concluding significantly: 'What attitude towards the Soviet regime can such a policy create in the people? Do not forget, comrades, that in many towns, there is still rationing.'[17] It therefore seems likely that the Party, in the same way as it is trying to create a 'Komsomol within the Komsomol' will attempt to form a new category of priest within the Orthodox Church, less obviously stooges of communism than the existing hierarchy and thus more effective in infiltrating believers. This seems to be presaged in an article in *Moscow News*:

Strict respect for legality in relations between the atheist state and the Orthodox Church implies a certain distance between them, necessary for both parties. This distancing could save the Church from the grave danger of suffocating in the toils of authority and, barred from spiritual independence, of becoming a department of state.[18]

Khartchev's speech is also interesting in that it reveals a total incomprehension of religion and faith. The historial and cultural relativism in the anti-religious propaganda to which Stalin resorted in order to counterbalance his 'concessions' to the Orthodox Church, has borne fruit. The Father of the People had declared: 'Obviously we are not very good Christians. But we must not deny the progressive role of Christianity at a certain stage.'[19] This 'culturalist' approach enabled faith to be reduced to folklore – a touching museum of popular traditions like pottery and weaving. Orthodox traditions are judged essentially positive, while the press overflows with criticism of Islamic habits and customs such as grandiose funerals and weddings, dowries, and so forth. The Orthodox Church embodies the great Russian patriotism with which the regime is conducting a discreet flirtation, recalling it as a factor in national unity, the battle against 'foreign invaders', and public morality.[20]

This 'enlightened' approach is highlighted by the attacks on it from various ideological dinosaurs who have complained about the 'flirtation with God' or warned against allowing an excessive amount of nationalism to seep into the ideological mixture. A. Yakovlev, for example, says

Render unto God the things which are God's; and unto the Church the things that are the Church's; and to us Marxists the fullness of truth. Beyond that, those who try to present Christianity as the matrix of Russian culture must be implacably refused.[21]

The new subtlety does not preclude cruder and more brutal methods of rooting out religion. In 1987 the official press mounted a virulent attack on the unregistered sects: Baptists, Seventh-day Adventists, Pentecostalists, and Jehovah's Witnesses are still a major enemy. Repression of the Uniates (Eastern Rite Catholics, numerous in the Western Ukraine despite systematic persecution since the 'voluntary' dissolution of the Church in 1946) continues unabated, while Eastern Rite Catholic churches have been ransacked by the police and even turned over to the Orthodox Church as happened in Kalynivka in 1988[22] and with the Gruchev Church, revered by the faithful as a place of apparition of the Virgin.[23] Catholic priests are subject to various continuing pressures, including arrest. Atheist indoctrination is being intensified in Galicia. The Uniate Church has still not been legalised, despite many petitions from Ukrainian Catholics, and the prospect of it seems to be receding.

The regime is particularly intolerant of any challenging of the official churches by their own members. In Latvia, for example, the press has launched a violent attack on the Lutheran 'Rebirth and Renewal' movement, which exposes the authorities' manipulation of the evangelical Lutheran Church. Non-registered sects are hated by the authorities as it is extremely difficult for the KGB to penetrate them or to put them to use for foreign policy. 'The existence of a large number of unregistered religious communities, particularly widespread in Central Asia and the Caucasus, cannot be tolerated. In these regions the religious situation is abnormal. . . . Self-proclaimed mullahs control religious and ritual practice and form opinion in a micro-group.'[24]

As regards the official churches, *perestroika* is indeed the order of the day. 'Self-management' has been imposed upon them, the idea being that they can best apply *perestroika* by bringing their own dissidents into line. At the Zagorsk symposium in December 1986, at which were gathered all the leaders and main functionaries of the official churches, the 'existence of dissident networks in this country' was deplored, and participants stressed that the church was 'empowered with the spiritual force' to heal them.

The official churches have been requested to police their flocks for dissidents who, 'in the ostensible cause of religious purity, compromise spiritual realities and are guilty of cutting the links they should be maintaining with their church.'[25] As Metropolitan Juvenal stated at a press conference on 5 June 1987, 'Just because current talk is of *glasnost* and *perestroika* does not mean there has to be anarchy in the church!' At the end of March 1988, shortly after its much-publicised meeting with Gorbachev, the assembly of Orthodox bishops in Moscow condemned dissidents in the Church.[26]

The churches could prove useful to the Communist Party in its campaign for the 'restoration of public morality' – notably in the anti-alcohol crusade and the drive to raise the birthrate in the Slavic regions. 'The different religions and their hierarchies, having recognised socialism as the most just social system, are appealing to believers to work honestly and conscientiously for the prosperity of the Soviet state. . . . The problems of atheist education have lost none of their topicality.'[27] The official churches can also contribute to the development of 'friendship between peoples'. The Armenian Catholicos, Vazgen the First, praised by *Izvestia* in October 1985 for extolling the 'humanism of the Russian people', appeared on Soviet television on 8 July 1988 taking 'internationalist' communion with Pashezade, Sheikh Ul-Islam, spiritual leader of the Transcaucasian Moslems. 'Internationalist' orientation of the official churches is more than ever necessary, due to 'the association of nationalist sentiments with religious feelings'.[28]

As in 1941, the Party remembers the Church when crises arise. After Chernobyl, *Literaturnaya Gazeta* opened its columns to Metropolitan Philaret, who took it upon himelf to explain to the panic-stricken population that the catastrophe did not signal the Apocalypse – the end of the world was not nigh. The recent reception at the Kremlin of the Russian Orthodox hierarchy indicates the gravity of the present situation in the Soviet Union. This flirtation with the Orthodox Church in no way signifies a wish to integrate with Europe (as propaganda meant for external consumption would have it), but on the contrary shows a determination to fight Western influence. With rare exceptions, the Orthodox Church has always stirred up hostility towards the West. On the 1100th anniversary of the death of Methodus,[29] *Literaturnaya Gazeta* recalled the persecution the Catholic Church inflicted on Cyril and Methodus (monks sent as missionaries to Moravia in 863, who translated the scriptures and liturgy into Slavonic and are believed to have invented the Cyrillic alphabet) and quoted Metropolitan Pankraty: 'The concept of a United Europe as the West understands it is not for us. . . . We are for a Europe in the spirit of Helsinki, a Europe of coexisting states with different political systems.'[30]

As far as foreign policy is concerned, the USSR has pressing reasons to launch an offensive on the religious front. The Soviets have always made great efforts to manipulate world opinion. Now, the Soviet state and its satellites have a greater than ever need for Western aid. The ruin of their economy has made it imperative for them to disarm the West, as they have had to abandon former hopes of winning the arms race. Traditional Soviet channels of influence like the foreign Communist parties have been discredited because of their all-too-evident close links with Moscow. It has become urgent to rethink the techniques of influencing world opinion and to regain the ground lost under Brezhnev. Wooing religious believers thus serves two goals of Soviet policy, one traditional, the other a reflection of Gorbachev's 'new thinking'.

The first goal is to establish diverse means of influencing international opinion. Countless foundations, organisations and institutes, are popping up like mushrooms everywhere, and their sole reason for being is to promote peace and disarmament, the latest slogans of the Communist propaganda machine. Clergymen look good in these organisations: thus

Metropolitan Pitirim is one of the leaders of the International Foundation for the Survival and the Development of Humanity, created in January 1988 in Moscow. Metropolitan Philaret is president of the Commission of Clergymen Struggling for Peace. Mother Teresa was received by Gennady Borovik, head of the Soviet Peace Committee. 'We are facing up to the vital task of concentrating our efforts to rid the earth and the heavens of nuclear weapons', declared Patriarch Pimen.[31]

The second goal is linked to the Soviet desire to 'change the image of the USSR' in Western minds, to encourage the non-Communist world to give up the stereotype of the 'enemy'. According to a pertinent analysis in *Literaturnaya Gazeta*,[32] the Western public's negative image of the USSR is based on the perception of the USSR as an expansionist, atheist and totalitarian state. Soviet propaganda has attacked these three representations with great skill and its usual consistency. In the United States, and above all in West Germany, the notion of the Soviet state as 'atheist' is being attacked. In his interviews in the American media, Gorbachev is constantly calling on God; he took care to be accompanied by Metropolitan Philaret to the summit meeting in Washington. In August 1987, at the Chatauqua Conference on Soviet–American relations, Metropolitan Juvenal and the Moscow Chief Rabbi, affirming that religious believers had no problems in the USSR, sounded the trumpets for *glasnost* and *perestroika*. In West Germany the Soviet Council of Evangelical Baptists was busy spreading the same message. At the World Hindu Conference Lama Chimit-Dorji Dugarov asserted that Buddhism in flourishing in Soviet Bouriasa.[33] The celebration of the Russian Christian millennium affords another opportunity for conferences and colloquia on *perestroika* and *glasnost* in the USSR and abroad. The international publicity campaign conducted for the millennium bears eloquent witness to the Soviet grip on world oipnion. Russia is not the only country in the world to have been converted to Christianity. But the USSR is the only one to have inveigled the international community into actively participating in hypocritical ceremonies commemorating Russia's conversion to the very Christianity that the Bolsheviks have done their utmost to destroy.

Gestures to churches therefore do nothing to indicate a real change in the attitude of the regime towards religion. Reactivation of the official churches and propaganda about their alleged 'independence' from the state signal, rather, a reactivation of the KGB, both internally and abroad.

In this time of crisis, the Party is resorting to increased manipulation of public opinion: clergymen are being solicited in the same way as scientists and other 'representatives of the intelligentsia'. With Marxism totally discredited, Leninist messianism is obliged to jump on other ideological bandwagons such as the fear of a nuclear apocalypse or the German Greens' rejection of Western civilisation. Recent developments show that the Leninists are even thinking of exploiting religion itself. The many religious persuasions in the USSR are invaluable world-wide transmission belts for

Soviet influence. 'We can say that today we see political cooperation with the Church as furthering our revolutionary goals', *Literaturnaya Gazeta* says proudly.[34]

The official churches may be permitted charitable activities. The example of Poland shows that this could be an important channel for free Western aid with no serious ideological after-effects. But changes in religious legislation can have no effect while the state of affairs persists that is described in this letter, published in *Glasnost*, from a Russian believer to Father Gleb Yakunin[35] (a dissident Orthodox priest, imprisoned in the Gulag and released under Gorbachev):

You recently sent a letter to the leaders of our country, proposing that they modify religious legislation. . . . Do you believe that a change in the laws, whatever it may be, will bring this about when the laws have never been observed? The main oppressor of the Church is the KGB, and what laws have any effect on that organisation? . . . Today the KGB has been assigned the job of recruiting all seminary entrants. . . .I don't understand how anyone can talk of freedom of the Church if tomorrow all the popes will be informers. What is is this 'free' Church? The real sickness of our Church today is that the hierarchy has sold out. This sickness is not confined to the head. Day after day, it is enveloping the entire Church, from top to bottom. . . . And, for contact with the foreigners, they have picked the super-Judases. End this perverting of the clergy by the sin of Judas – this is the main demand that people like you ought to make to the authorities.

Asked about the present attitude of the Soviet regime to the church, the dissident young Orthodox priest Vladimir Chibaev replied:

They intend to destroy the Church. To destroy it, pure and simple. The form changes: before, they used terror above all else; today they are destroying the Church, all the churches, from the inside. . . . This is even more terrible. It is now the chief weapon of atheistic power, this working from the inside.

If its treatment of the churches is a guide to the nature of *perestroika*, Father Chibaev's remarks are food for thought.

NOTES

1. See P. Henk in *Est et Ouest*, no. 51, February 1988.
2. 7 December 1977.
3. *Pravda*, 11 June 1988.
4. *Pravda*, 2 February 1988.
5. *Pravda*, 28 January 1988.
6. Peasant (or rustic) authors were the first to condemn the long-term effects of collectivisation. Their ideal is the patriarchal and agricultural Russia of the old days, to which they contrast the depraved, destructive, urbanised and

Westernised modern life. The most famous of these writers are Valentin Rasputin, Viktor Astafiev and Vasily Bielov.

7. *Pravda*, 2 February 1988.
8. *Communist of the Armed Forces*, no. 10, May 1988, p. 27.
9. 19 November 1986.
10. No. 10, May 1988, p. 29.
11. *Communist of the Armed Forces*, January 1988, no. 2, pp. 59–61.
12. *ibid.*
13. *Communist of the Armed Forces*, May 1988, no. 10, p. 26.
14. *ibid.*, p. 30.
15. *ibid.*, p. 31.
16. *ibid.*, p. 32.
17. *Pensée Russe* 20 May 1988.
18. 19 June 1988.
19. Quoted in *Moscow News*, 7 August 1988.
20. See *LG*, 12 June 1985 and 9 September 1987.
21. *Bulletin of the Academy of Sciences*, no. 6, 1987.
22. *Ukrainian Press Service Bulletin*, no. 3, March 1988.
23. *Pravda*, 29 July 1988.
24. *LG*, 18 May 1988.
25. *La Croix*, 15 January 1987.
26. *RLRB*, 6 April 1988.
27. *LG*, 18 May 1988.
28. *Pravda*, 8 April 1987.
29. *LG*, 25 July 1986.
30. 29 May 1985.
31. *Pravda*, 2 February 1988.
32. 28 October 1987.
33. *RLRB*, 6 April 1988.
34. 18 May 1988.
35. *Pravda*, 29 April 1988.

5. Nationalism

Some time ago the West was astonished – and a little frightened – to find that the nationalist passions of the nineteenth century, which took two ruinous world wars to exorcise, had not altogether vanished from Europe. In the Communist world nationalist passions continued to smoulder, notwithstanding all the rhetoric about 'class solidarity'. Recent events have shown that the 'internationalism' beloved of official Communist ideologists remains a fiction as far removed from the truth as all the other tenets of socialism.

What caused the current explosion of nationalism in the USSR? Gorbachevian 'social scientists' proclaim that *perestroika* is not to blame for this outbreak. The roots of the present troubles, they say, lie in Stalin's 'distortions' of Leninist national policy, and in the 'system of administrative command' introduced in the 1930s and culminating in the Brezhnev 'stagnation'. Nationalism in the USSR (and in the entire Communist bloc) does indeed have deep roots, but the situation is more complex than the ideologists would have us believe. The official explanations are interesting, none the less, as they reveal the framework of future policy.

On the nationalist issue, Soviet ideologists still resort to the classic Marxist principles now abandoned in other areas. Outbreaks of nationalism have socioeconomic causes, as the press points out at great length. Neglect of the social sector under Stalin and Brezhnev resulted in housing and medical shortages, a decline in the provision of staple foods, and so forth. Social injustice stood out more blatantly against this stark background.

Furthermore, the injustices have proliferated of late. Local mafias are quite out of control, and favouritism in allocating housing and places in higher education has bred understandable grievances in the population. Added to this has been the neglect of certain 'socio-cultural needs' of national minorities. Instead of cultivating 'friendship between peoples', local intelligentsia formed under Soviet rule have fanned nationalism. 'The experience of Azerbaijan and Armenia shows to what extent certain representatives of the intelligentsia can play a fatal role.'[1] In Kazakhstan and Uzbekistan, 'reactionary moments of the past have been idealised'[2] by historians and novelists. In Uzbekistan the anti religious struggle was neglected to the point where 'atheists were being persecuted' and CPSU members themselves were having mosques built.[3] All these problems were swept under the carpet during the 'period of stagnation'. When Moscow attempted to clean up the mess, 'corrupt elements' whipped up nationalist sentiment and launched 'extremists' on to the streets, provoking the present troubles.

This is the first line of interpretation of recent events, formulated after the Alma-Ata riots precipitated in December 1986 by the sacking of the First Secretary of the Kazakh Communist Party, Kunayev – a Kazakh – and his replacement by Kolbin, a Russian. In 1988 a second line was introduced, incorporating criticism of the 'system of administrative command' which is now identified with the 'braking mechanisms' afflicting Soviet society. The republics suffer from economic over-centralisation in the same way as the enterprises. They are subject to the pillage of requisitioning and then have to beg funds from the central authorities, which puts them in the humiliating position of eternal supplicants. It is right, asked an Estonian delegate at the 19th CPSU conference, for the central ministries in Estonia to have control of 90 per cent of the republic's economic potential? And is it acceptable, asked a Turkmen delegate, that Turkmen enterprises return 530 million roubles to the federal treasury, while the central authorities allocate only 344 million to Turkmenistan?

These genuine complaints should not serve to disguise the essential fact that nationalism is an implicit rejection of the Communist system. This can be seen in the speed with which the Armenians have abandoned 'perestroikist' slogans for much more radical demands. The Estonian parliament is meanwhile demanding the restoration of private property as well as sovereignty for the republic.

The Gorbachevites are therefore wrong to say that *glasnost* has had no effect on the recent explosion of nationalism. The effect on the Byelorussians of the discovery of mass graves in Kurapaty near Minsk, where the NKVD slaughtered hundreds of thousands between 1937 and 1941, cannot be underestimated. Similar mass graves have been uncovered in the Ukraine and in Moscow. Eyewitness accounts of the massacres were published in the press. The authorities are vainly hoping that Stalinism will bear the full blame for these crimes. The growing popularity of Solzhenitsyn in the USSR demonstrates that the notion of a good Lenin vs. an evil Stalin is losing ground. The peoples composing the USSR (including the Russian people) are re-examining the horrific events of their recent history, characterised by massive exterminations, terror, famine and deceit, in the light of a distant past that must seem idyllic by comparison.

In these circumstances the revival of nationalism is hardly surprising, nor is the fact that it expresses itself in rejection of Soviet symbols. The national flag has not only been raised in the Baltic states, but also in Byelorussia and even in Leningrad, before a cheering crowd of 15,000.[4] The publication in the Baltic states of the secret protocol of the Molotov–Ribbentrop pact, drawing a dividing line between Russian and German spheres of influence in Europe, only reinforced the idea of the illegitimacy of the Soviet regime. By denouncing the notion of 'collective responsibility' used to justify the mass post-war deportations of whole peoples accused of having collaborated with the Germans, *glasnost* encouraged the Crimean Tartars to reassert claims to the ancestral territory.

The ecological problems revealed by *glasnost* have also contributed to the renascence of national consciousness. Here again, everyone, including the Russians, has reasons to feel victimised. The Ukrainians saw Chernobyl and the proposed installation of new nuclear plants in the Ukraine as a sequel to the enforced collectivisation of the 1930s – in other words another genocide by Moscow of the Ukrainian people.[5] This was shown by an appeal – launched by the representatives of democratic national movements who met at Riga on 24 and 25 September 1988 – against the Soviet nuclear power programme, in their eyes more dangerous for Europe than Soviet military power.[6] 'The arrogance and indifference of certain federal bodies, in particular the Ministry of Energy, with regard to the Ukraine, are not only cruelty but an affront to national dignity,'declared the Ukrainian writer Boris Oleinik at the 19th CPSU conference. 'What is national egotism? If the Komi republic protests about the waste of national resources . . . is that egotism or patriotism?' 'It is not only a question of indifference to national interests: we risk quite simply finding ourselves soon on a bare earth,' added another delegate.

The Estonians have fiercely resisted the proposed exploitation of a phosphorous mine on their territory; they fear a new influx of Russian migrants and see the project as a means of reinforcing the Russification of Estonia. The inhabitants of Riga strongly opposed the construction of an Underground in their city for the same reason. In Kazakhstan the Popular Front is equally worried by the proposed construction of an Underground which would require the billeting of 10,000 Russians on Alma-Ata.[7] In Armenia ecological issues were from the beginning associated with the Karabakh (an Armenian enclave of Azerbaijan) troubles, and the first demonstrations of October 1987 were against the pollution of Yerevan by, among other things, a rubber factory. The Uzbeks are accusing the Russians of having imposed on them a single-crop cotton culture, thereby ruining the soil, and of destroying the health of their women and children with butifos, a particularly toxic defoliant finally outlawed in 1987. Azerbaijanis are complaining that they are forced to make wine grapes their principal crop (accounting for half the republic's revenue) to the detriment of other, more urgently needed produce.[8] The proposed diversion of Siberian rivers to Central Asia caused a general outcry in Russia and was finally abandoned, much to the disappointment of the Uzbeks who protested strongly against the decision.

Hypercentralisation of the economy is beginning to prove dangerous to Moscow, where all local grievances invariably end up; and ecological conflicts soon take on nationalist overtones. The republics do not see why they should have to suffer the ecological consequences of projects managed by a federal Ministry which bring nothing into the local economy and poison the air and water of the region. The East Europeans have clearly seen the absurdity of a planned economy which consumes enormous resources, increasingly pollutes the environment and does nothing to raise the living standards of the local population. This sense of waste and absurdity is at the heart of the ecological/nationalist conflict in the Communist world.

There is a basic ambivalence in the nationalism of Soviet bloc countries. Generally speaking, nationalist pressures would seem to endanger the Communist empire – and what happed in Alma-Ata, the Armenian and Georgian demonstrations, the Baltic nationalist movements are certainly worrying to the authorities. None the less, the regime would far, far rather deal with nationalist fervour than with a concerted political opposition. It is much better for the CPSU to have the Russians accused of every imaginable evil, in the Soviet Union as well as in the satellite nations – and to have the Russians blaming the Jews for the plagues that have fallen on Russia – than to be confronted with a sudden realisation among the subject peoples that communism is entirely responsible.

Nationalism is a release, dangerous but controllable, for the long years' accumulation of grievances. Between communism and nationalism there is deep affinity. Both subsitute symbols for reality, and neither is 'political' in the Western sense. Nationalism breeds forms of opposition which communism can handle: the commemorative Masses of post-Solidarnosc Poland, the demonstrations on symbolic dates, the flowers laid on monuments to those killed. All these rituals provide an *ersatz* political existence occupying the crowds without noticeably compromising the Communist order. The Communist authorities in Eastern Europe have resigned themselves to the existence of nationalism and are trying to make the best of it. Nationalism abounds in false issues (it has been seen to what extent the Russian intellectual scene has been sterilised by 'Slavophile' polemic), arouses easy hatreds and can slide rapidly into the grotesque. The Communist authorities can then take a virtuous role presenting themselves as champions of moderation, reason and enlightenment. If there were no Pamyat* movement, the CPSU would have had to invent it.

Nevertheless, there has been a boomerang effect, even in this area. In seeking to reduce nationalism to a simple formula with essential 'socialist' content, in plain words to dissipate it in folk dances, pottery and restoration of churches and ruins, the regime has transformed nationalist passions (just as it has with religious feeling) into idolatry. Idolatry, which has no room for reasoned argument, breeds fanaticism. Just as Communists are constantly rooting out heresy, so nationalists work on principles of exclusion and revere icons which serve as rallying-points. This attitude, while so similar to Bolshevism, is now turning against it.

National animosities are raging out of control because the political arena that could have contained them has been destroyed. This has led to the recent massacres, notably those in Sumgayit in March 1988, when young Azeris slaughtered several hundred Armenians. Nor has nationalist violence

---

*Pamyat is an 'informal association' of Russian nationalists, notorious for its anti-semitism and anti-Westernism. It claims several million members, and there are numerous indications that it enjoys some Party support.

been confined to Transcaucasia. Even in Moscow there have been bloody street-fights between Russians and young Central Asians. On 20 February 1988 300 Russian youths attacked 200 Uzbeks in Petchatniki, a suburb of the capital. There were at least ten deaths.[9] The regime thus risks outbursts of naked violence which it will not be able to contain except with the special forces of the Ministry of the Interior. Though quite ready to exploit the fear of pogroms to promote 'stability', i.e. reinforcement of central power, it sees the threat posed to its existence by the explosion of nationalism. Ever since the Alma-Ata riots, therefore, the regime has been assiduously developing means of coping with the present crisis and considering how to prevent nationalist conflicts in the long term.

DEFUSING THE CRISES

Consulted by the CPSU Central Committee on the question of Armenian territorial claims, the Institute of Oriental Studies offered these recommendations:

The Commission [created to consider the Karabakh question] must, insofar as possible, play for time while examining the question. The return of Karabakh to Armenia is undesirable. The population must be placated by concessions in the cultural, social and daily domain; if necessary a portion of the leadership must be sacrificed and of course lower-level culprits sought out. Nevertheless, the High Karabakh must not be returned to Armenia. An impression of total *glasnost* must now be created, in contrast to the previous period. The smallest affronts must be highlighted and blamed on the Armenians. We must infiltrate the Armenians as far as possible, making use of the Kurds in particular, who are the best-disposed towards the Armenians of those who live in Armenian territory, while attempts must be made at the same time to destroy this friendly relationship.[10]

This passage could serve as a handy introduction to the regime's manual of crisis management. The same methods were used in Kazakhstan, Karabakh and with the Crimean Tartars. An interview with Gennady Kolbin, the 'normaliser'; of Kazakhstan, published in *Literaturnaya Gazeta*,[11] completes the list of recommendations:

• To play for time in the hope that things will calm down, that militant fervour will diminish and give the other measures adopted a chance to bear fruit. The Gromyko Commission, charged with examining the territorial claims of Crimean Tartars, took months to announce a decision which must have been taken in advance.

• To throw responsibility on to local authorities, blamed for the disgraceful state of the 'social sphere', neglect of 'internationalist education'; and corruption. Nationalist flare-ups are always followed by purges in the region concerned. It is by no means certain that the purges teleprompted by Moscow enjoy the support of the population. In Uzbekistan the investigators sent by the central authorities were 'surrounded by a climate of hostility and incessant provocations'[12] which seemed, more than the normal obstructiveness of cadres under inspection, to stem from collective resistance. Local authorities employ various means of reprisal, such as announcing that the shops are empty because the central Ministries have taken everything,[13] or that 'they are unable to better their people's standard of living for fear of being accused of nationalism.'[14]

• To put sausage in the shops, build houses, and convert into kindergartens a few dachas misappropriated by local functionaries. As federal resources are scanty and cannot cover all the 'pressure points' in the USSR, there is no course open but to follow the cynical advice of *Communist of the Armed Forces*:

The consequences of unfavourable social conditions need not mean insuperable difficulties for the policy regarding nationalities. It is possible to attenuate them considerably and even to eradicate them, but on one condition: there must be a just national policy down to the smallest detail.[15]

It is enough therefore to share hardship equally among all the ethnic groups.
• To isolate eventual nationalist leaders and get rid of them, by forced emigration or arrest. Gorbachev, a good Leninist, knows that a movement is only dangerous when it becomes an organisation, in other words when it acquires leaders. The authorities are taking great pains to prevent 'informal' associations from becoming 'formal' ones. Or, if this proves inevitable, to bring them under the wing of the Party. 'We are far from indifferent to the question of finding out who will assume the role of informal leaders,' declared Kolbin candidly. Talaka, the patriotic Byelorussian association, has been analysed in the local press:

There must be good judgement and recognition that the leading 'quartet' is not to be confused with the ordinary members of Talaka, who are genuinely concerned (like all the workers of the republic) by the necessity of preserving the assets of the national culture, and are far from having overt nationalist ambitions.[16]

Through the various 'popular fronts', the CPSU is hoping to 'channel the energy of the masses into concrete actions',[17] harmless from the official point of view. 'Groups of benign enthusiasts have an extremely important role to play in the attenuation of mass passions. . .when the administrative and directivist levers have ceased to function, the popular movement remains, for the most part, under control – auto-democratic control.' [18]

Official propaganda supports this tactic, distinguishing between the inexperienced mass, 'politically immature' but nursing genuine grievances about the negligence of local functionaries, and the 'self-proclaimed leaders', 'extremists' seeking 'from pure personal ambition' to 'make political capital' and obviously in the pay of the CIA and other hostile secret services. 'Socially useful activities' are contrasted with the diatribes of demagogues. In the *Literaturnaya Gazeta* interviews with Kolbyn, the journalist mentioned complaints about the Party from 'informal groups' that 'you are purposely pushing us into building houses and clearing cellars to keep us from politics'. Kolbin replied: 'Outrageous! According to them, growing wheat, building houses, looking after orphans and the sick – that is not politics. Let me say loudly and clearly that we already have enough windbags like that!'

• To satisfy the 'cultural needs' of national minorities and channel nationalist demands in harmless directions such as preservation of language, restoration of historic monuments, and so forth.

• To set local minorities against the main national group. In the Baltic states, various recently-created internationalist movements combine Russians, Jews and Poles in opposition to the Popular Fronts dominated by native Balts. This 'divide and rule' policy is highly dangerous, as can be seen in Transcaucasia today, and may well have a boomerang effect that the authorities will regret. Anti-Semitism is often produced to discredit a national movement. In May 1987 propagandists of the Kiev Komsomol spread rumours that the Ukrainian Culturological Club[19] was planning pogroms. Meanwhile, the press was accusing the club of Zionism, having discovered some Jews among its leaders.[20] Even with Pamyat, it is questionable whether the KGB is not encouraging the anti-Semitic outbursts and various lunacies highlighted by the official press. The regime has as much to fear from genuine Russian patriotism as from that of other nationalities. What would happen if the Russians demanded an end to the empire which has ruined them, and to the messianic ideology which has bled them white? The authorities' reluctance to publish Solzhenitsyn probably stems from this, as he calls on Russia to withdraw into itself to lick its wounds, to regain its own freedom by lifting the yoke of communism from its subject peoples. It would be interesting to study the 'national policies' of Pamyat, which condemned the invasion of Afghanistan and sided, at least partly, with the territorial claims of Crimean Tartars. Pamyat strikes a strong chord among Russians. It would be surprising if the authorities were not manipulating the movement, making it into a monster to terrify the West and liberal Russian intellectuals and locking it into grotesque debates (like the one between the 'pagans', who consider the original conversion of Russia to Christianity as the first stage of the Jewish plot against the Slavic peoples, and the 'Orthodoxes', defending the notion of Moscow as the third Rome).

• To set the population against the nationalist 'extremists', with the help of the media and rumours spread by the KGB. This last element often goes unnoticed in the West – a great mistake, as the KGB has made an art of the use of rumour, both at home and abroad. As Grigoriantz, Editor-in-Chief of the independent review *Glasnost*, says:

Rumours that Crimean Tartars were planning a massacre of children surfaced simultaneously in the Crimea, the Krasnodar region and Central Asia. The authorities and school directors began advising parents to keep their children at home. According to other rumours, the Sebastopol police gave instructions to local police volunteers and announced that young Crimeans had been killed by Tartars, and that the Tartars had sent five boatloads of armaments which were intercepted by KGB troops. I mention this to further understanding of what is happening today in Azerbaijan.[21]

It should be remembered that the Sumgayit pogroms were set off by a rumour of the murder of two Aziris by Armenians. The media are pursuing the same objective – to isolate troublemakers – but under cover of speeches disingenuously quoted from outraged workers, such as a letter from a war veteran published in *Pravda*:

I was born and raised in Karabakh. I worked and became a CPSU member there. The fate of my compatriots matters to me, even though I have moved away to Baku. This is the first time I ever read in the papers that the workers of a region have purposely failed to fulfil the targets of the plan. It's shameful . . . who will compensate for the state's losses? Where are you, veterans, Communists, Komsomol? Could our fathers and forefathers ever have dreamt that their descendants would renege on their obligations to their brothers in other republics like this? My dear friends, aren't you ashamed? How can we ever forget that the USSR is our common home.'

Pravda, to drive the point home, added: 'The correspondent is right. The strike fever will cost us and *perestroika* dearly. . . . It is a terrible blow to the country's economy . . . losses are already being counted in the hundreds of millions.' [22]

The Armenian strikers have been presented as opportunists placing their own parochial ambitions above the common interest, blinded by nationalist passions and engaged in 'a ruthless exploitation of *perestroika*'.[23] Appeals to *perestroika* are a constant blackmail, not only in the USSR but in the entire Communist bloc. Polish strikers are called upon to resume work to avoid endangering Soviet reforms and lending support to Gorbachev's hawkish adversaries. 'The present conflict in Moscow between supporters of reform and conservatives is the most important element in the socialist world since Lenin. . . . People do not engage in revolution when there is a chance of evolution,' says *Solidarnosc* adviser Adam Michnik.[24] Reform (or the promise of it) has become an important factor in preserving the status quo in the Communist bloc, a means of imposing self-censorship and self-restraint on all potential opposition, including nationalist opposition. Curiously, this type of propaganda seems more effective in the satellite countries than within the Soviet Union. The Estonian parliament had no hesitation in demanding sovereignty, while the Polish opposition still does not dare to call publicly for an end to communism, for fear of compromising 'dialogue' and 'round-table discussions'.

The lessons for the Party of these recent events is that it must act in good time. As Kolbin says:

The Party's work consists in giving political leadership to social initiatives. Political leadership begins with a political appreciation of the situation, as all subsequent decisions depend on this initial appreciation. . . . Social initiative must be in keeping with a correct political appreciation. And here there must be no fear of displeasing some people. Complacency with regard to politically immature tendencies causes a fatal aggravation of inter-ethnic relations.

It is too soon to seek to evaluate the success of these techniques. There has been no crisis in Kazakhstan since the Alma-Ata riots, but the press indicates that the situation still leaves much to be desired. Karabakh was a total débâcle, even in the opinion of Volski, the proconsul sent from Moscow who, in his report to the Supreme Soviet, expressed himself shocked by the gross ingratitude of the region's inhabitants:

The decisions of the CPSU Central Committee and All-Union Council of Ministers concerning the High Karabakh are beginning to be put into effect. This has enabled some improvement of the situation in socio-economic development; the isolation of the Armenian sector of the population from Armenia in terms of language, culture and education is being gradually overcome. . . . We might say without fear of exaggeration, comrades, that in any other region of the country these measures would have been welcomed thankfully. . . . Yet this has not been the case in Karabakh [where] emotion has overwhelmed reason. . . . In this context the socio-economic measures have themselves been devalued.[25]

To judge by comments from officials and the press, the federal authorities feel that the purges never go far enough. According to Volski:

The clans in Azerbaijan and Armenia have maintained a hold on many levers of power. The leaders that they have shaped and promoted continue to exert an influence on the local atmosphere and to affect many decisions behind the scenes . . . in the two republics we are seeing an increase in the role of corrupt and mischievous characters. . . . And certain Party and government organs, unhappily, flirt with them and sometimes leave the initiative to them, forgetting principle. This is why a stronger emphasis must be put on purge processes.

The authorities seem aware of the limitations of the methods used up to now to defuse nationalist crises, and understand the necessity of developing a long-term strategy.

DILEMMAS AND HESITATIONS IN NATIONAL STRATEGY

The Gorbachev line is rarely so contradictory as on the question of 'centralisation' and 'decentralisation'. For instance, in Warsaw Gorbachev declared: 'While ridding ourselves of over-centralisation and the bureaucracy it breeds, we are in favour of a strong central power, without which no modern society can exist.' [26] The regime has evidently not as yet decided a policy in this area and is wavering between opposing alternatives. The general aim is clear: to create an integrated socialist society. The debate concerns the means of achieving it. The theoreticians, as good Marxists, understand the political role of the economy as a factor in integration. The experience of the EEC has given them food for thought. The idea is therefore to give wide-ranging autonomy to grass-roots economic organisations and municipal and local authorities in order to avoid reinforcing structures at republic level, the load on which had already been considerably lightened by the 'struggle against bureaucracy'. 'Self-accounting' (*khozraschet*) at republic level was widely supported, mostly by regional Party leaders. 'This principle has much to recommend it as it will enable the application at regional level of the motto of socialism: from each according to his ability, to each according to his labour,' emphasised a Baltic delegate at the 19th CPSU Conference, not without mischief. But 'enlightened' Gorbachevites also see self-accounting as being in Moscow's interest. In August 1988 Alexander Yakovlev declared in Riga: 'The solution to the problems of the country's socio-economic development can best be achieved through national forms.' Regional *khozraschet* 'constitutes a genuine obstacle to nationalist tendencies', said *Pravda* at the same time.[27] This system would enable local authorities to be blamed for various 'inadequacies', whereas at present the grievances invariably rebound on Moscow. Each republic compares its payments to the federal treasury with the money it receives from the centre, and each feels itself cheated. Each one feels that it is paying for all the others.

On the other hand, the federal authorities are apparently recoiling from the probable consequences of regional 'self-accounting'. During his visit to Latvia and Lithuania in September 1988, Yakovlev said explicitly that Moscow was not ready to take the decision. The stumbling-block is unquestionably the problem of currency and ownership. The Estonian parliament had voted through an amendment stipulating that the soil and resources of the Estonian republic were exclusively the property of the republic. Gorbachev's reaction was:

To raise the question of the transfer of goods common to the Soviet people to the profit of a single republic is a serious theoretical and political mistake. That would topple the unique economic base of socialist society, destroying the possibility of a single and consistent social and economic policy, of rational distribution of productive forces, of creating single systems of transport and energy. Is it reasonable to push towards autarchy and an insular economy when integration, division of labour and cooperation are the main objective trends in the world? The fact that, in these documents which are the object of the discussion today, private ownership is admitted along with other forms of ownership, concerns us particularly. By plurality of ownership we mean the diversity of socialist forms. . . . To want to re-establish [private ownership] indicates regression, and is a profoundly erroneous decision. . . . It is essential to be consistent in the furthering of economic integration processes. . . .

Complete self-management is not possible except in the largest link of the chain; that is, the enterprise which is the socialist producer. Enterprises cannot belong to a republic or to a Ministry, whether in Moscow or Tallin.[28]

Those who imagine that the option of decentralisation opens the door to parochialism and selfishness are greatly mistaken.[29]

Pravda is even more explicit:

Now more than ever, the interests of the federal and autonomous republics require not weakening but reinforcement of central power. Recent experience has shown that dissension between republics can take a bitter and tragic form. It is likely that a move to regional *khozraschet* will, at least at first, provoke a whole series of new conflicts threatening to destroy our common home. Only a sufficiently competent supreme power can decide these conflicts in a just and impartial manner.[30]

The same article uses the argument of the 'current trend towards global interdependence of humanity' to attack the idea of a possible confederation (why wish to 'transform our powerful federation into a wimpish confederation?'). Gorbachevian ideologists, conscious of the shaky legitimacy of Leninism, are devising alibis invoking the laws, institutions and developments of the non-Communist world to justify decisions aimed at maintaining and reinforcing the Communist order. The same procedure could be seen in Poland when the Gdansk factory closures – a purely political measure – were presented to the world as an economic step of 'Thatcherite' inspiration.

In the view of the Soviet authorities, economic integration will also help to combat the current demographic trend towards ethnic homogeneity in the republics (the Baltic states excepted) which Moscow is observing with a baleful eye. There are now more Kazakhs than Slavs in Kazakstan because the Kazakhs have a higher birthrate and Russians are leaving the republic. Transcaucasia is experiencing the same thing, whereas at the turn of the century Tiflis and Baku were completely cosmopolitan cities. The political leadership recognises the dangers of this: 'To claim that the population of the republics should become nationally homogeneous is to create obstacles to the objective processes of internationalisation in our life.' [31]

Soviet authorities obviously consider now that national policy must be discriminating. The Baltic states are the principal beneficiaries of this 'new thinking'. The door to the Western wing of the 'European home' must not appear – to the West – a prison door. An interesting *Pravda* article recalls Lenin's criticisms of Bolshevik policy in Georgia. As Georgia was 'the single Soviet republic with traditional commercial links to the capitalist world through Batum', it was necessary to 'make economic use of the capitalist world in a swift and intensive manner', even at the price of 'greater tolerance of all sorts of *petit bourgeois* elements . . . who were not absolutely hostile to the idea of the Soviet regime'.[32]

Gorbachev and his supporters hoped to be able to harness the nationalist issue to *perestroika*, making it, to borrow Yakovlev's phrase, 'an additional moving force of *perestroika*'.[33] When the leadership launched purges in the local Party apparatus, it attempted first to gain the support of the local intelligentsia – with variable success, as has been seen. Thus, *glasnost* – at the beginning of 1986 confined to the Russian media – quickly won over the press in the republics. Everywhere authors previously accused of 'bourgeois nationalism' were being rehabilitated, and everywhere Stalin's crimes were denounced. Moscow had concluded that the feeling of having lived through a common historical tragedy could only bring people together. But even here, some were more equal than others. *Glasnost* was restricted in the Ukraine, as the Gorbachevites were reluctant to attack Shcherbitsky (the Ukrainian First Party Secretary inherited from the Brezhnev era). The Editor-in-Chief of *Ogonyok*, Vitaly Korotich, himself a Ukrainian, justified maintaining the Breznevian status quo in the Ukraine in these terms:

The situation is rather sad and anti-democratic, but a civil war is the last thing Gorbachev needs. *Ogonyok* launched the theme of corruption in Uzbekistan – a republic of no great strategic importance – and you saw the upheaval that followed. I am not sure that from a strategic point of view it would be opportune to raise the subject of the Ukraine.[34]

The Ukrainian national press has several times accused Ukrainian nationalists of planning another Sumgayit.

It may be that the Soviet authorities are playing the role of the sorcerer's apprentice in raising so many hopes among the peoples of the USSR. It is impossible to apply a differentiated, Chinese-style regional policy in a country which is not a nation at all, as was shown by the speed with which the Georgian Supreme Soviet adopted demands identical to those of the Baltic states. Already, the regional media and intelligentsia are showing alarming signs of independence. Before the 19th CPSU Conference, one of the leaders of the Kirghiz Writers' Union, Kazat Akmatov, expressed the wish that the federal constitutional article stipulating the 'leading role of the Party' should be repealed. The Kirghizians are seeing *perestroika* as a pretext for Russia to 'jump down their throats'. They are contrasting the grand ceremonies celebrating the millennium of Christianity in Russia with the accusations the official press rains down on Islam.[35] A Kirghiz literary review has decided to publish some chapters of *The Gulag Archipelago*.[36]

The press in the Baltic states published the secret protocol of the Molotov–Ribbentrop Pact, while the central press was still doubting its very existence. The Chief Prosecutor of Latvia has complained that the Latvian media, with the exception of two organs, 'effectively escape all Party influence and control' and that 'we are witnessing a very similar situation in Estonia'.[37] The Ukrainian railwaymen's journal has published an article by Solzhenitsyn entitled *Live Not a Lie*.

With regard to state institutions, Gorbachevite functionaries have been most astute in limiting the implications of Soviet demographic evolution on the representation for non-Russians in the Congress of People's Deputies and the Supreme Soviet. The addition to the Congress of 750 Deputies elected by mass organisations (presumably most of these are Russians, as the organisations must exist at federal level to have the right to elect Deputies to the Congress, which excludes the various national Popular Fronts from representation) will dilute the non-Russian element. It was planned to change the composition of the Soviet of Nations to comprise seven Deputies from each federal republic, four from each autonomous republic, two from each autonomous region and one from each autonomous district. This would have decreased the proportion of Deputies elected by the federal republics from 64 per cent to 50 per cent, and increased that of those elected by the RSFSR and its territorial dependencies from 32 per cent to 43 per cent.[38] However, opposition to the proposal from the republics was so strong that Moscow retreated. The number of Deputies elected by each republic will now remain unchanged, while representation of the RSFSR and its dependencies will rise only 3 per cent to a total of 35 per cent.[39]

Other changes have also been criticised. Henceforth the Supreme Soviet 'will determine the legal status of social organisations' (Article 73.9) – i.e. the Popular Fronts. 'The Supreme Soviet will proclaim martial law or a state of emergency in specific regions or the country as a whole, introducing special forms of administration if necessary. . . .' The Balts have interpreted this as a legal licence to the Presidium to get rid of regional authorities at will.[40]

Without Terror, the Leninist–Stalinist policy of satisfying nationalist feelings with Houses of Culture, regional costumes and restoration of historic monuments cannot remain effective for long. This can be seen in the rapid evolution of patriotic 'informal associations' which begin by busying themselves with old churches and pottery but progress quickly to political demands which are much more worrying to the regime. But while the nationalist factor destabilises Communist power in the long term, it can also have a totally opposite effect. It reactivates Leninism in the elites of the leadership and freezes ideological discourse. 'We have understood one obvious thing: we who are so diverse have only one common path: genuine scientific socialism,' says the 'Soviet Kipling', Alexander Prokhanov.[41] 'We are first and foremost Communists, and only secondly representatives of this or that nationality', declares Academician Primakov.[42] Lenin's comment is invoked that 'No Marxist . . . can deny that the interests of socialism must override the rights of nations to self-determination.' [43] If the USSR were a nation instead of an empire, 'de-ideologisation' would not be constantly hindered by the fear of losing colonies. The Russian people pay with their own servitude for the captivity of subject nations. *Glasnost*, so forward in denouncing Stalin's crimes, has not yet dared to ask the fundamental question: do the Russians think it has all been worth it? Do the Russian people share the 'state stoicism' (acceptance of Bolshevism for the sake of state power) preached by Prokhanov? The opposition in Russia is deeply divided and often confused on this issue. Some movements, such as the recently-created Democratic Union, seem to recognise that freedom for Russia will follow from emancipation of the other nations. The most dangerous element in the current Soviet political scene is the combination of the messianic Russian nationalism, exacerbated by the catastrophic state of the country, with a Leninism which has been revamped and has redis-covered its former aggression.

The following remarks of Academician Likhatchev are significant: 'Only by being aware of our responsibilities world-wide can we other Russians preserve our leading role in our country's situation.' [44] The Communist empire is never internally stable except when expanding. To have as neighbours free countries aware of and strong in their freedom is pro-foundly destabilisi8ng for a totalitarian state. Internal national tensions therefore do not necessarily make Soviet foreign policy less dangerous or ambitious, as many in the West imagine. Quite the contrary. The present extremely unstable equilibrium cannot last. Either the militant ardour and renewed taste for liberty of the outlying nations will spread to Russia, or the climate will change to another long frozen winter for Eastern Europe.

NOTES

1. G. Borovik, XIXth CPSU Conference.
2. *Communist of the Armed Forces*, no. 18, September 1988, p. 84.
3. *Pravda*, 6 September 1987; 5 February 1988.
4. *The Times*, 12 October 1988.
5. Some extracts from a tract published by the Ukrainian patriotic association 'Heritage' and 'Society':

   It is time to limit the predatory management of our country. Originally we were obliged to take pride in being the breadbasket of Russia. Then we became the forge and furnace of the entire Soviet Union. Today the Ukraine is becoming the pan-Soviet nuclear reactor, with the prospect of becoming the pan-Soviet or even world graveyard. . . . *Glasnost* revealed in our newspapers the truth of the terrible 1930s . . . the truth about the 8 million victims of the artificial famine of 1933. But the truth today – where is it, why do they want to hide it from us? The truth about the 7.5 million people among us who will die before their time in the next ten years. . . ? And this because of a single reactor at Chernobyl. But fifty of them are being imposed on us! (*Ukrainian Press Service Bulletin*, no. 11, November 1988).

6. *RLRB*, 2 November 1988. Ukrainian, Armenian, Georgian, Latvian, Lithuanian, Estonian, Moldavian and Crimean Tartar representatives were present.
7. *LG*, 7 December 1988.
8. *Pravda*, 13 February 1988.
9. *Pensée Russe*, 11 March 1988.
10. *PR, 18 March 1988.*
11. *December 1988.*
12. *Moscow News*, 30 October 1988.
13. *Pravda*, 24 May 1988.
14. *LG*, 7 December 1988.
15. No. 10, May 1988.
16. *Sovietskaya Byelorussia*, 19 October 1988.
17. According to the expression of an Estonian Communist functionary. See *Moscow News*, 31 July 1988.
18. *Moscow News*, 2 October 1988.
19. A Ukrainian nationalist association, very badly regarded by the authorities.
20. *PR*, 3 June 1988.
21. *PR*, 18 March 1988.
22. *Pravda*, 18 July 1988.
23. *LG*, 10 August 1988.
24. *Radio Free Europe Research*, 6 May 1988.
25. 1 December 1988.
26. 11 July 1988.
27. 30 August 1988.
28. Speech to the Supreme Soviet Presidium session, 26 November 1988.
29. Speech to the XIXth CPSU Conference.
30. *Pravda*, 23 November 1988.
31. *Communist of the Armed Forces*, no. 18, September 1988, p. 17.
32. 8 July 1988.
33. *RLRB*, 14 September 1988.
34. *RLRB*, 5 September 1988.
35. *RLRB*, 20 July 1988.
36. *RLRB*, 12 October 1988.
37. *Pravda*, 23 November 1988.
38. *RLRB*, 9 November 1988.
40. *RLRB*, 23 November 1988.
41. *LG*, 10 August 1988.
42. *PR*, 5 August 1988.
43. *LG*, 24 August 1988.
44. *RLRB*, 26 October 1988.

6. *Perestroika* in international relations

Those who remain sceptical about Gorbachev's 'new thinking' are nowadays crying in the wilderness. Did Shevardnadze not recently declare that peaceful coexistence is not after all a form of class struggle, that 'the battle between two opposing systems is no longer a decisive tendency of our era'?[1] Even more recently, Georgy Arbatov wrote in *Moscow News*[2] that 'this idea [of the struggle of opposing systems] was mistaken, as it projected the laws of internal development on to international relations mechanically and simplistically . . . those who made a fetish of class struggle were not Marxists but ignoramuses and sectarians.' During the period of 'stagnation' this kind of statement would have been heresy. Taken out of context, it seems a startling breach with Leninist doctrine. But this is misleading.

It was Lenin himself who advised against raising the topic of world revolution in diplomatic settings, as *Literaturnaya Gazeta*[3] recalls. The ideological journal of the military, *Communist of the Armed Forces*, has quoted Lenin's dictum that 'Revolutionary phraseology must be combatted at all costs, so that the bitter truth that "revolutionary phraseology about the revolutionary war has lost the revolution" will never be applied to us'.[4] *Pravda*[5] recalls Lenin's advice on the eve of the Hague peace conference organised by the socialists:

Through all the inevitable compromises, we must remain true to our principles, our class and our revolutionary mission. . . . It is quite inexcusable to endanger an extremely important practical undertaking for the pleasure of one more polemic. . . . Communists must not just stew in their own juice, but learn to introduce themselves into 'restricted areas' where the *bourgeoisie* has influence over the workers, without fearing to make sacrifices, without fear of the inevitable errors at the outset of any difficult new undertaking.

Yuri Zhukov commented on the quotation:

The decision taken by our Party leadership to attend the Conference bore fruit. While it was difficult for the Soviet delegation to defend its views in this restricted area (to borrow Lenin's phrase) where the Communists had succeeded in introducing themselves (to be sure, only under the banner of trade unionism), they were able . . . to air their basic detailed programme, which had long-term consequences in international relations at non-governmental level.

The Leninist tone of Zhukov's remark is striking.

A salient characteristic of official Soviet declarations and analyses is their colossal global ambition and messianic pretension. These more than anything else bear witness to the persistence of the Leninist perspective. The USSR is constantly assuming the role of spokesman for mankind and prophet of the future. It is *perestroika* which has renewed its licence to do this as, thanks to 'reform', the USSR is now delighted to find itself once again in the vanguard of progress. It seems that foreign policy consider-ations may now be overriding the original domestic motivation of *peres-troika*, which

cannot but raise the level of spirituality in the whole world. . . . Highly interesting perspectives on the struggle for the minds of people and public opinion are being opened. . . . Democratisation and *glasnost* are becoming an effective instrument of foreign policy.[6]

Without wishing to offend our American guests, I believe that the Moscow summit has confirmed the intellectual leadership of the USSR in approaches to problems of global policy.[7]

Perestroika offers new possibilities to Communists in countries where capitalism still reigns.[8]

The Leninist adverb 'still' is significant.

New realities . . . create additional conditions for a new phase of our revolution. The historic mission of the forces of socialism, democracy and progress consists in reinforcing existing realities [i.e. the conquests of socialism] and creating new ones which will form an insurmountable obstacle to the forces of aggression and intervention. This is precisely what the USSR is accomplishing with its *perestroika*. The successes of the latter are the basis of our international successes.[9]

I would like to emphasise the extremely close links which exist between the domestic and foreign policy of the USSR. The renewal and development of our society are a sound launching-pad to increase our influence in international affairs and the interests of peace and security, the interests of socialism.[10]

In short, 'our policy of *perestroika* has enabled us to achieve successes in foreign policy such as we have not had for 30 years.' [11]

It is worth looking closer, through the Soviet press, at this loudly-proclaimed renunciation of class struggle in international relations and ostensible preoccupation with the 'common interests of humanity' and the 'unity' of the human race, and at these attempts to 'link the cause of global human problems with the class struggle'.[12] 'Our class interests coincide completely with the paramount interests of humanity.' [13] 'We are internatio-nalists and the fate of no country, no people is unimportant to us.'[14] 'World unity is built on the foundation of Marxist–Leninist values, and the revolutionary process is the spearhead of these values.' 'By its very nature socialism is called upon to carry on the fight for the good of humanity, which enables it to realise its humanist mission of world renewal. It is thus that the proletariat overcomes the obstacles to its own interests.' [15]

These passages leave no doubt that the traditional Leninist rhetoric has been shelved for the sake of Leninism. Furthermore, the Soviet presumption to speak in the name of mankind shows that Moscow has not abandoned its totalitarian plans. It may be that the CPSU, forced to make domestic concessions, is compensating for this unwelcome necessity by redoubling its foreign ambitions. Already, *perestroika* and *glasnost* are being held up as examples for the whole world to follow. The United States 'would do well to look at its history and itself in the same spirit of openness with which we are examining our past.' [16]

It is we and not they (the USA) who have proclaimed and are realising *perestroika* . . . it is we who have kept a critical appointment with history. In the West they are living as they have always lived with their problems and complacency. Ours is the bolder venture . . . we have found ourselves in the extremely responsible position of initiators . . . which intensifies the mechanism of world interaction and affects . . . the foreign policy of the United States.[17]

Soviet democracy is becoming a model to which to aspire. 'We are frequently reminded that a single-party system does not ensure authentic democracy: however, a comparison between the 19th Party Conference and the Atlanta [Democratic] convention is unflattering to the latter.' [18] 'The whole world must engage in *perestroika*.' [19] Mankind is condemning those who remain 'prisoners of stereotype', 'cold warriors' locked in 'Manicheism'.

However, Gorbachevian foreign policy is facing new constraints. The Soviet regime has never been so dependent on international aid for its survival, and never so aware of it. It becomes clearer every day that the Communist economies are incurable (as long as they remain Communist) and that the 'reforms' are only accelerating the decline. There is only one hope for the regimes in power: to convince the free world to subsidise the socialist bloc and its Third World colonies. Their main objective now is to plug the Communist anti-economies into the world market and persuade the international community, by diplomacy or intimidation, to consent to Communist parasitism. 'The renewal of all forms of our social life is closely linked to *perestroika* in international relations.' [20] Hence the accent on 'interdependence'.

As Gorbachev says, 'we are condemned to cooperation.' [21] In a remarkable article in *Pravda*,[22] Yevgeny Primakov has written that 'Never before has the organic link between domestic and foreign policy been so clear as it is today. [The report of the 27th Congress] corrected the distorted notion by which the confrontation of the two world systems was envisaged as separate from their mutual dependence.' Lenin was opposed to the 'export of revolution', but never considered accepting the 'social status quo'. Primakov concluded that confrontation must not occur at state level. The USSR has no intention of exporting revolution and indeed has never done so, according to the official press. 'Ever since Lenin, non-interference in the internal affairs of states has constituted an important part of our domestic policy,' declared Gromyko to the Filipino Senator Oliver Mercado.[23] But that cannot prevent people from launching themselves towards socialism, as that is the tide of history. Within this Leninist frame of reference, calls for 'de-ideologicisation of relations between states' are perfectly consistent. As *Pravda* recently stated, 'Before, over-ideologicisation hindered our actions in the international arena.' [24] The Soviet state is ready to cooperate with all other states. It is not its fault if the inhabitants of other states spontaneously 'choose' socialism.

The term 'new thinking' thus has two different applications which must be distinguished in order to understand towards which 'new world order' the USSR is tending. On one hand, the proclamation of the 'new thinking' is itself an instrument of foreign policy. Like *glasnost*, it aims to demonstrate a fundamental breach between past practices of the Communist regime and its present attitude. Its object is to make peoples and governments forget past experience of Bolshevism and re-set the dial at zero; to lead the West to abandon the doctrine of 'containment' and the 'stereotype of the enemy' (which the West never formed – it is a singular Gorbachevite impertinence to draw parallels between the legitimate suspicions of the non-Communist nations towards a country which deals in betrayal, and the pejorative 'imperialist' stereotype cultivated and reinforced by official propaganda for 70 years in the Communist world). On the other hand, the 'new thinking' has inspired a number of changes – not in strategy or the Leninist *weltanschauung*, but in Soviet tactics of diplomacy. The 'new thinking' is an excellent example of 'the creative application of Marxism–Leninism to analysis of the realities of the nuclear age, with the purpose of establishing correct class strategy and tactics.' [25]

PRINCIPLES OF THE NEW THINKING

The Soviets, in the process of drawing up an account of their past history, are permitting daily press criticism of domestic policy. Foreign policy is judged far less severely (though reservations are expressed from time to time). As Gorbachev has said, 'despite some errors and miscalculations in the past, Soviet foreign policy has done enormous service to the country and to socialism, to all humanity.' [26] It is nevertheless interesting to see which accusations are levelled at pre-Gorbachev diplomacy, as these show in negative the orientation of the new thinking. Stalin is blamed for not having fully exploited the possibilities of the 'anti-Hitler coalition' and for having left the way open for a Western alliance against the Soviet Union. 'When a state wishes to undertake a crude enlargement of its sphere of influence, other states unite in an 'anti-coalition' against the real or potentially dominant state . . . rejection of expansionist tendencies provokes hesitations in, and the collapse of, the anti-coalition.' [27]

The USSR has advertised its role as head of the international Communist movement too openly, so much so that

the leading NATO circles have viewed all the progressive processes of socialism exclusively through the prism of modification of the global political equilibrium in the Soviet Union's favour. This has made the activities of progressive forces in the zone of capitalism and the developing world very difficult. . . .[28]

It is now fashionable to criticise the deployment of the SS-20s and the invasion of Afghanistan, condemned as having resulted from an 'over-estimation of the possibilities of the USSR' and an 'underestimation of international resistance';[29] and as provoking a Western reaction which 'placed the Soviet Union in an extremely difficult position with regard to foreign policy and the economy.'[30] In other words, the condemnation is from a purely Leninist viewpoint. Under Breznev, 'there was no clear idea of the real national state interests of the USSR. These interests did not consist in seeking basic minimal and formal gains, such as *coups d'état* in developing countries. . . . Foreign policy was exhausted through enormous waste.'[31] All this is even more unpardonable because

if in 1917 it was possible to break the chain of imperialism in a single country without external help, it can be said that now the conditions for transition to socialism on the national scene are infinitely more favourable . . . today socialism has become an irresistible force. That is why it is important that the centre of gravity in the battle for social progress [i.e. the extension of Communism] should pass from the sphere of inter-state relations between USSR and the West to the sphere of sociopolitical development within the USSR, the socialist countries, and Western and Third-World countries.' [32]

Criticism of foreign policy is strangely similar to that of domestic policy. The CPSU has sought to impose itself too much from outside, with purely authoritarian methods. It has neglected the Leninist principles of entryism and mass organisation, lost Lenin's genius for timing and forgotten that it is sometimes better to let things take their course, waiting for the right time to act, than to exhaust its energy on costly schemes. Over-centralisation has led it to sacrifice its real power to the pursuit of hollow triumphs. It has been too obtrusive, operating openly on occasions which required more discretion. It has often alarmed the West and provoked reactions which would have been easy to avoid. The principles of the 'new thinking' can be traced through this retrospective criticism. Henceforth the USSR must take more care.

It must establish priorities in its objectives; accept sacrifices if necessary (like every good chess player); and ensure that the majority of sacrifices are of a symbolic order, while the gains are tangible and real – for example, by ending Sakharov's internal exile, rehabilitating Bukharin, saying a few kind words about Trotsky, and releasing a few political prisoners in return for

Western credit and disarmament. Ex-President Nixon is the only Western politician to have realised the dangers inherent in this: 'If we reward Moscow every time the Soviet press shows up the problems of the USSR, Moscow will accumulate strategic gains while we collect newspaper cuttings.' [33]

It must not put all its eggs in one basket: this may have been the lesson learnt from the defeat in Afghanistan. The Soviets are evidently regretting having moved too fast in the communisation of Afganistan, skipping the 'popular front' phase which had traditionally paved the way for Sovietisation of popular democracies. Instead of depending solely on the Afghan Communists, the Soviets should have sought out non-Communist allies as well.

The same error was committed in diplomacy. 'Previously, the establishment of relations with one country led to our breaking them with one or more others. Today we have left that idea behind,' declared Krasnov, Director of Middle Eastern affairs at the Novosti Press Agency.[34] Yevgeny Primakov has given the Americans a piece of fatherly advice to avoid making the same mistake of supporting only the Afghan rebels without contemplating a coalition.

The results of this change of policy are already apparent. Instead of having to depend only on Cuba, the USSR is making advances throughout Latin America. Instead of entertaining only long-standing Middle-Eastern clients such as Syria and the PLO, it is making contacts with 'moderate' Arab countries and even with Israel. Instead of having political capital exclusively in national Communist Parties, which are losing ground, it has launched a campaign to seduce social-democratic and – why not? – Conservative parties. This is not to say that Moscow is sacrificing its faithful Communist retainers, neglecting their interests or relaxing its grip on them: quite the contrary. Courtship of the Western nations is being accompanied by increased attempts at integration of the COMECON countries, all disguised by rhetoric urging the right of each nation to choose its own path to socialism.

The USSR must make the most of its own weaknesses and setbacks. It has been seen how the revelation of past crimes has become an instrument of foreign policy and is now increasing Gorbachev's personal prestige. Chernobyl and the Armenian earthquake have provided official propaganda with new arguments for the 'supremacy of common human values'. The military defeat in Afghanistan has been transformed into a diplomatic trump card. The necessity, for demographic reasons, of cutting back the armed forces is presented as a gesture of unilateral disarmament, a gift from Gorbachev to NATO. The resurgence of nationalism is attributed to the 'liberalism' of *perestroika*, and so forth. In true Leninist fashion, the USSR is attempting to transform a basic vulnerability (its dependence on the goodwill of others) into a means of extending the influence of socialism, in other words into another trump.

The march of history towards progress, today as never before, is not achieved only by the passage of new countries to a higher level of social existence [i.e. to socialism] but also by an increase in mutual ties between the peoples on the surface of the planet, by an enlargement of economic, political and cultural links.[35]
Our task is to find forms of interaction [between capitalism and socialism] which will enable socialism to participate more actively in the process of world development and the international division of labour, while conserving the socialist principle and increasing its influence.[36]

'The establishment of normal business relations with states of opposing systems disarms anti-Sovietism, and thus anti-communism, thereby weakening the pressure of reaction to democratic [i.e. Communist] exertions and conquests.'[37] 'International relations, without losing their class nature, are becoming increasingly relations between peoples.'[38] The enforced 'opening up' of the USSR thus offers new possibilities for Soviet propaganda and will allow the Soviets access to previously restricted areas.

Last and most important, foreign policy must be made 'self-accounting'. Shevardnadze says that 'We must increase the profitability of our external policy and strive for a situation in which our mutual relations with other states will be a minimal burden on our economy.'[39]

Verbal concessions do not therefore imply an essential change in the Soviet worldview, but rather a better perception of the actual possibilities for the USSR, and the restrictions it must take into account in its activities abroad. Furthermore, it often transpires on closer inspection that apparent concessions are really no such thing. Behind all the talk of 'cooperation', hostility to the United States remains constant. The intention of weakening and isolating the Western democracies is still ever-present, in speeches as well as actions. *Pravda* said recently that 'socialism is a movement towards the perfecting of human existence. And every obstacle to this movement must be destroyed.'[40] And 'military disarmament does not mean ideological disarmament.'[41]

THE OBJECTIVES OF *DÉTENTE*

It has been pointed out that the main reason for *détente* is to get credit and technology from the more advanced countries. But *détente* under Gorbachev has other motives that were not there under Brezhnev (or were present to a lesser degree).

The first of these is to impose self-censorship on the non-Communist world. At a time of weakening Communist power and increasing crisis within the Communist bloc, it has become essential to find some means of leading the West to limit itself whilst lending a hand, economically and even ideologically, in the running of the Communist empire. Peoples under communism have to be shown that the regime has the West (and the rest of the world) behind it. During the Moscow summit, the official press reported with relish that President Reagan had renounced his idea of the USSR as an 'evil empire'. This was presented as a Western capitulation and then used to demoralise citizens of Communist bloc countries. Many examples demonstrate that the Soviets see *detente* and the signing of accords as a way of imposing self-censorship on their adversaries. Thus, Reagan's appeal to demolish the Berlin Wall was condemned as contrary to the spirit of *detente*,[42] which shows to what extent the Soviets see '*detente*' as Western acceptance of their point of view. *Voice of America* programmes devoted to the nationalist troubles in the USSR were declared 'contrary to the spirit of the Washington agreements'.[43] From the moment the US signs a treaty with the USSR, it must refrain from 'provoking' its 'partner' by showing too much interest in Soviet internal affairs. *Voice of America* was sternly advised to get on with its own *perestroika*.[44]

In periods of *detente*, Soviet spies should be left to do their job without hindrance from the host country. When Canada had the cheek to expel certain over-curious Soviet 'diplomats', *Moscow News* saw it as 'a shot fired from the trenches of the Cold War'.[45] The slightest sign of self-protection by a democracy is immediately stigmatised by Communist propaganda as deriving from a 'Cold War mentality', the extremely pejorative connotation of this term being also largely due to the efforts of the same Communist propaganda. 'Besides nuclear and conventional disarmament, we must promote a psychological disarmament, gradually overcoming the stereotypes of the "enemy".'[46] Much more than Brezhnevian *detente*, Gorbachev's '*perestroika*' *in international relations* is aimed at weakening the will of the non-Communist world to resist communism. Its object is – more than to provide the USSR with material aid – to associate the international community in the upkeep and eventual expansion of Soviet domination. What Moscow really means by 'cooperation' can be seen from such shining examples of it which were praised in the official press, such as the Finnish–Soviet publishing house which publishes texts provided by the Soviets, with the Finns paying for paper and production. Or the recently-established review *Our Heritage*, which is 'prepared in Moscow and printed in London'.[47] And what of the recent offer by the Soviets to transport across their territory all Western aid destined for Afghanistan[48] which would give the Soviets a formidable means of influencing the country they have devastated? There is no better illustration of the principle of 'self-accounting foreign policy' and 'new thinking', by which the assets of the West are made to serve Communist power.

These days, the Soviets are emphasising that their adversary is no longer 'capitalism' as such, but 'militarism'.[49] Some good can come from capitalism, on condition that it submits entirely to the will of the Soviet Union; that is, on condition that the capitalists are deprived of any means of self-defence. The USSR now realises that imposition of communism on the world would result in global famine. It is therefore resigned to the existence of capitalism in 'reservations': various 'Hong Kongs' to be scattered throughout the Communist empire. It is thus that Gorbachev's speech to the UNO on 7 December 1988 must be understood. 'Internal processes of transformation' [i.e. evolution of countries towards socialism] cannot achieve their national aims if they develop in isolation without using the assets of the surrounding environment. In other words, without foreign aid it is impossible to build communism. The Soviet press has hailed the Soviet–Finnish relationship as a 'model of cooperation between states' demonstrating the 'realistic nature of the idea of *perestroika* in international relations'.[50] Nothing could be clearer.

THE POLICY OF *DÉTENTE*

The Soviets are taking pains to create a momentum favourable to *détente* in the international media, in arms control negotiations, international exchanges, diplomacy, and so forth. The aim is to persuade social organisations, political parties and individuals to trust Gorbachev the reformer, and to build up in the West an immense pro-Gorbachev lobby oblivious to factual evidence.

Before every major CPSU gathering, Western journalists are thrown into a frenzy of speculation on the imminent 'revolutionary measures' to be introduced by Gorbachev. When the mountain is revealed as a molehill (as was the case with his speech on the 70th anniversary of the October Revolution, his trips to Prague and Warsaw, and the 19th Party Conference), those journalists are obliged to find mitigation in vague promises of even more radical reform at the next Party convention, or in the 'resistance' of 'conservatives'. They will never face facts and recognise that their enthusiasm was premature. This accounts for Western interest in the rhetoric rather than the reality of *perestroika*, which suits the Soviets perfectly.

Diplomats fall into the same trap when signing agreements with the USSR. They prefer to let Communist infringements pass in silence that then to admit themselves duped. After the assassination of General Zia, an American State Department official was quick to exonerate the Soviets from suspicion, though the question of Soviet involvement should certainly have been raised – especially in the light of declarations such as Shevardnadze's on 7 August 1988:

We are prepared to take all measures to ensure that upholding of the Geneva accords by one side [the USSR and the Communist government of Afghanistan] and their flagrant violation by the other side [Pakistan and the United States] do not create problems in the Republic of Afghanistan. We have not only the right but the duty to ensure the upholding of accords.

Fear of unpleasant discoveries even led the US State Department to forbid an FBI investigation at the site of the plane crash.[51]

In arms control, the Soviets are following the same tactic of momentum-creation. *Pravda*[52] has quoted Kalevi Sorsa, vice-president of the Socialist International: 'The American elections will halt the disarmament process for at least a year.' 'Europe, the UN, and political movements' must therefore take the initiative. Last August *Pravda*[53] was saying that 'there must be no pause in the course of disarmament. An advance in one area must lead to others in other directions.' Shevardnadze's opinion of the INF treaty (eliminating medium-range missiles in Europe) is that 'elementary arithmetic does not always faithfully reflect the strategic equilibrium, especially from the viewpoint of its evolution. It is true that we have destroyed a larger number of missiles. But the real return will be measured by the final tally of reductions.'[54] Each Western country prompts its allies to conform to its own attitude towards the East, in other words to negotiate with the Soviets. The weakness of one country justifies that of the next. The same thing occurred in the 1930s with Hitler, when the French excused their own debility with reference to British blindness. The USSR has not forgotten that lesson. France is consenting to disarmament so as not to compromise the Franco-German alliance. West Germany is using the INF treaty to demand new reductions in its own forces. Finally, NATO will concur in the common desire for disarmament. Moscow knows that in order to topple its adversaries it must first crack the combination of the American lock. Once the Americans can be presented as 'partners' of the USSR, the rest of the West is sure to drift toward Soviet objectives. Moscow has accordingly been seeking an 'American alliance'.

GORBACHEV'S AMERICAN POLICY

Current Soviet policy towards the United States is modelled on the 'anti-Hitler coalition', the wartime Soviet–American alliance which brought the USSR substantial material and territorial gains. General Yazov has recalled the era with nostalgia:

Among the many lessons for the present and future which the victory gave to humanity, there was one which contained the seed of today's policy of new thinking: namely that, faced with Fascist enslavement, alliance between capitalist states and a socialist country was possible. The atmosphere of cooperation among the countries entering into the anti-Hitler coalition, the genuine comprehension of the new situation which appeared after the smashing of Fascism, were reflected in the post-war accords, which answered the interests of peace. By the fault of Western reactionary circles, the experience of cooperation has been forgotten.[55]

The Soviets have come to the conclusion that 'without the United States, it will be impossible to do anything in the area of security either in Europe or in other regions.'[56] 'We believe that the progress of Soviet–American relations constitutes the key to all the rest.'[57] Alliance with the Americans is a prerequisite to any change in the European situation favourable to Soviet interests, just as in 1945. With the United States showing the way, the other NATO countries cannot but be responsive to Soviet initiatives in disarmament and other areas. 'The efforts of the USSR and the United Staters must be complemented by multilateral efforts.'[58] 'The development of Soviet–American relations and the signing of the INF treaty have created a new situation in Europe . . . new means have appeared of attaining our objectives in foreign policy.'[59] 'The very fact of the Soviet–American alliance has a considerable effect on mankind's perception of the world.' [60]

The Soviets have much to gain by making the world believe that they and the Americans are 'natural allies'.[61] It gives them a chance to advise other countries to copy the USA. For example, Ryzhkov has told the President of the Mitsubishi corporation that 'the potential of Soviet–Japanese relations has not been realised to the full. This is particularly evident against the background of the USSR's relations with many Western countries, including the United States.' [62] Pravda reported the remarks of the Filipino Senator O. Mercado: 'Even the United States has accepted the re-establishment of joint ventures and commercial exchanges with the USSR. But we Filipinos remain attached to our prejudices.' [63] By proclaiming their friendship with the USA from the rooftops, the Soviets are pursuing two objectives always in mind when Communists form a coalition with a non-Communist partner: to reinforce communism and discredit the partner. In this respect, the role of the United States resembles that of the Orthodox Church.

The model of the 'anti-Hitler coalition' is also evident in regional conflicts. Mindful of Yalta, the USSR is promising coalition governments and free elections on condition that the United States stops supporting anti-Communist resistance. It is essential to interpret the sovspeak correctly to understand what the Soviets mean by 'liquidating the sources of tension'. Tension (or 'confrontation', another common term in Gorbachevian discourse) exists because of resistance to communism. The best way to end the tension is to stop resisting. The people themselves will choose socialism. The United States alone refuses to respect this choice, seeking to hinder the 'democratic process' and provoking 'tensions'. 'Interference in internal processes in order to impose another course on them would be destructive to the shaping of world order,' said Gorbachev in his speech to the UNO on 7 December 1988. 'The cause [of Soviet–American disagreement about regional conflicts] is that the United States does not readily accept the fundamental principle of free choice for each country.'[64] 'The internal collisions in Nicaragua would long since have been resolved if the United States were not pouring oil on the flames . . . by supporting the Contras.'[65] National 'reconciliation' is impossible unless all foreign aid is denied to the anti-Communists: 'The success of the cause of national reconciliation [in Nicaragua] depends considerably on Washington's policies.'[66] African National Congress President Oliver Tambo is more specific: 'World peace requires us to find a rapid solution to regional conflicts, eliminating by force or diplomacy the causes and the sources of these conflicts.'[67] Naim Ashkab of the Palestinian Communist Party is just as clear:

The time has passed when national liberation movements and anti-imperialist movements . . . considered that *détente* between states, particularly between the USSR and the United States, hindered their struggle. The concrete experience of the 1970s confirms that international *détente* creates favourable conditions for a reinforcement of national liberation struggles.[68]

As *Pravda*[69] said about Pakistan 'Is it right to count on differences between Moscow and Washington? These are of varying magnitude.'

The Soviets now generally prefer to deal with collective bodies, as these can be manipulated in the same way as 'mass organisations'. The USSR hopes to see NATO tranformed little by little into an organisation for disarmament and East–West cooperation and a West European conduit for Soviet influence on the United States.

Unfortunately, the Soviet Union and the socialist countries sought, at the Helsinki Conference in 1975, to exclude the United States and Canada from future European processes. Happily, we have only shortly highlighted this unrealistic and frankly damaging position . . . the participation of the United States in the future system of European security is necessary and natural. However, we do not think that United States military presence on the old continent should remain at its present high level. . . . The participation of the United States in the system of European security will enable the European powers to maintain an influence – mostly for good – on United States military strategy. Experience has proven that the influence of the European allies, the fear of losing their support . . . have more than once helped to restrain Washington from launching or persisting in adventurist actions.[70]

Gorbachev's NATO project envisages two phases: first, the total disarmament of the Alliance, making it an empty shell into which the Soviets can inject a filling of their choice; and secondly, once NATO is to Europe what Contadora is to Latin America, the USSR hopes to make it another tool with which to pressurise the United States.

Rather than indicating a change of attitude towards the United States, recent Soviet statements reveal Moscow's new ideas for its international strategy, the aim being always to weaken the United States by whatever possible means. But the USSR has realised that military might plays a lesser role than it had thought in the potential of a nation for world influence. It has seen the importance of the economic factor. Moscow wishes to neutralise *all* the American means of influence. As there is no hope of arriving at economic parity with the West, some other device must be found.

The solution hit upon by Gorbachev leadership is summed up by one of the main slogans of 'new thinking': 'democratisation of international relations'. knowing Communist newspeak by experience, the French translate 'democratisation' as 'influence gained by the Communist Party'. It is as well to keep this in mind when considering Gorbachev's proposed 'democratisation of international relations'.

As a first step in 'democratisation', Moscow has made a show of renouncing its 'superpower status' [71] and taking its place in the rank and file of the 'international community', embracing the interests of mankind. Naturally it accepts the role of spokesman for humanity. Commenting on the 3rd UN General Assembly session, when the United States vetoed an Indian proposal to forbid military use of new technology, the Soviet Vice-Minister for Foreign Affairs, V. Petrovsky, declared: 'The priorities of Soviet foreign policy coincide entirely with the priorities of the international community . . . the United States has shown that it places its own interests above those of the international community . . . which understands very well that it is necessary to take action . . . to place the interests of humanity above national interests.' [72]

The speech given by Y. Kvisinsky to the 19th CPSU Conference contains the best description of the current Soviet position:

We have seized the initiative in the international arena and have retained it . . . we must continue energetically . . . in the contemporary world the position of one state is determined by a group of factors of which the most important is economic power. This is frequently used by the other side to achieve its foreign policy objectives. In any event, much more frequently than military power. . . . We have not succeeded in attaining parity in the economic domain. . . . Consequently . . . at every opportunity the questions must be raised of prohibiting the abuse of economic power, of the danger of its use in international relations, of the establishment of an international control on the use of economic levers, and of the distribution of superfluous economic resources which exceed the normal needs of a state and its population to those in the international community who have need of them.

The USSR is thus trying to entangle the USA in a network of international organisations manipulated by the Soviet bloc and its allies. In doing so, it is waging 'class war' at international level, using all the usual slogans of the Communist movement and other terms aimed more specifically at fitting the international community to the pattern of a mass organisation.

We therefore find 'equality among states' linked to denuclearisation ('the liquidation of nuclear arms is an important step towards authentic democratisation of relations between states, towards their equality' [73]; or appeals – such as Shevardnadze's in his recent UNESCO speech – to fight against 'the tendency to monopolise scientific-technical applications', which Gorbachev echoed by proposing 'rational repartition of the assets of the scientific-technical revolution'.[74] Everything that allows the United States to maintain a semblance of a foreign policy must be eliminated. According to

Moscow News,[75] the problem of arms dealing should be raised by the UNO, as the United States depends on its arms trade to 'win friends and influence people' abroad. The Soviets understand that 'unilateral actions in foreign policy are generally less effective'.[76] Rather than striving to remain a 'superpower', they now elect for solidarity with the proletariat of the international community, being naturally the vanguard of this, as yet unawakened, 'mass'. The aim of this manoeuvre, formulated with startling crudity by G. Arbatov, is 'to place the United States in the situation of outcasts in the international community'.[78] It is evident that Arbatov is accurately expressing the current Party line and not his personal fantasies, especially as *Pravda* has stated that 'The world is indivisible and consists of mutual relations. It remains to be seen how the United States will behave in the new conditions, when the new thinking gathers strength.'[78] External pressures can therefore neutralise 'imperialism'. 'The laws of the world in its globality can limit the action zone of the narrow class interests of monopolist capitalism and block the most dangerous tendencies of the predatory nature of imperialism.'[79]

Regional organisations are the best environment for furthering the 'democratisation of international relations'. Soviet satellites and dependants are doing their best to upset the 'correlation of forces' within these organisations. Cuba, for example, used the theme of debt to launch a great diplomatic offensive against the Contadora group, which resulted in the execution of a complete about-face by several countries (notably Costa Rica and Guatemala) with regard to the Sandinistas. In May 1987 Vietnam was requested to set about seducing ASEAN, where Soviet anti-nuclear rhetoric is now gathering force. In the Middle East the USSR is going all out to create an Arab front united on an 'anti-imperialist basis' under the direction of a reconciled Syria and PLO. In his speech on the 70th anniversary of the October Revolution, Gorbachev gave a list of regional organisations the increased 'autonomy' of which compensated, in his eyes, for the decline of national liberation movements. This interest in regional blocs is not a part of the 'new thinking' as such. Rather, Moscow has decided to follow up previous military gains with diplomatic incursions. The Helsinki model is being extended to the rest of the world.

EUROPEAN POLICY

The USSR is actively preparing for 1992. According to Soviet experts,

This process [Western European integration] may exacerbate the structural differences between the economic complexes of East and West and in the long term complicate the development of their economic contacts, as well as the international division of labour on the continent. It cannot be excluded that a relative extension of the internal market of EEC member countries would lessen their interest in the East

European market. . . . Thus the intensification of Western European integration may lead objectively to aggravation of division on the continent.[80]

This complication may be remedied by increasing contacts between the EEC and COMECON but 'only the dismantling of the mechanisms of military confrontation is likely to prevent the negative effects on East–West relations of the formation of a single EEC market.' [81]

'In the past we did not always correctly anticipate the perspectives of the development of Europe and her capacity for integration,' say Soviet analysts. According to them, there are two possible models for European development: either denuclearisation from the Atlantic to the Urals, with multilateral cooperation; or West European maintenance of nuclear arms, with a revived Western European Union (EUO) as the pillar of a 'reformed' NATO. The current leadership has opted for the second as the most likely. Economic and political integration is leading to military integration. France is 'making the most effort' in this area, but is not supported by British suspicions of Franco-German military cooperation.[83] In his speech to the 19th Party Conference, Kvisinsky stated:

The process of political and military integration of the West European countries is making great strides. A great change is imminent in the disposition of forces. The USSR has noted these realities and drawn conclusions in its approach to the EEC. . . . Much will depend on what the EEC decides to be – an additional prop of the NATO bloc in Europe or a factor in a new European thinking, for construction of a common European home. And much will depend on us . . . if there is no real integration [in Eastern Europe], a growing number of European states may be snapped up by the EEC, and thereby NATO. In other words, we will have the construction of a North Atlantic Order instead of development of equal cooperation of our two systems on a common European base.

Gorbachev has said to the Italian Communist Natta that 'we are not considering the processes of West European integration only in a critical way, we are looking at all their aspects. The only thing we fear is attempts to militarise these processes.' [83]

From the Soviet viewpoint, there are various potential disadvantages of European integration.

The worst eventuality would of course be a strong and united Europe with military and political links to the United States. Western European integration might reunite West Germany and its Western neighbours. The prospect of Franco-German military cooperation is a gloomy one for Moscow. 'We can see the risk in Europe of the appearance of forces dangerous to the USSR and its Third World allies.'[84] Western European military integration is highly undesirable, particularly under the NATO umbrella. Soviet determination to disarm Western Europe, when by all accounts they see no real threat from the Alliance, and to compensate for the economic reinforcement of the EEC by dismantling Western defence, should be arousing extreme suspicion in Western Europe. Why are the Soviets so eager to deal with a disarmed but prosperous Europe?

Nevertheless, a unified Western Europe would be easy to manipulate, always in the cause of 'democratisation'. The USSR therefore takes an interest in small West European countries such as Denmark, Luxemburg and even San Marino, and in courting them assiduously. In the ideal Europe from the Soviet point of view Moscow would maintain its grip on the Soviet satellites, particularly East Germany:

Today it is the political realities that are important. There are two German states with differing sociopolitical systems. This state of things must be preserved in the interests of stability and construction of a common European home which cannot be based except on the social choice made by each people.[85]

But Western Europe would be in charge of supplies (Gorbachev said in Poland that 'the common European home must have a common material foundation if it is to be solid and comfortable for everyone'[86]), providing the East with transport and energy and rectifying ecological disasters, not forgetting the transfer of technology.[87] Shevardnadze could not have been more frank with Genscher when he called for the abolition of 'artificial limitations on economic cooperation, particularly the COCOM lists and EEC quotas . . . which would create conditions enabling the technological division of Europe to be overcome.'[88]

Does this mean that the Soviets have forsaken their political designs on Western Europe? 'Certainly many barriers still exist preventing union of the two Europes. But the nuclear barrier has been reduced from both sides before our eyes . . . henceforth the road is open for extensive cooperation between the "two Europes".'[89] In *Moscow News*[90] Austrian Foreign Minister Alois Mock has made favourable mention of 'pan-European integration'. A recent *Pravda* article[91] throws some light on the future European strategy of the USSR. Criticising the Gaullist notion of a Europe caught between two superpowers, the article states that in fact Europe is a unit, the uniting factor being none other than socialism.

The influence of Europe in the world cannot but be lessened by its division into political–military blocs, caused by the initiative of the Western leaders of the time who were uneasy at the East European people's choice of socialism . . . the socialist vision of the world has become a part of European tradition.

The 'common European home' should follow the rule of 'democratic self-denial', i.e. self-limitation and distribution of resources to the more needy.[92] In an interview in *Literaturnaya Gazeta*,[93] the Swiss sociologist, Jean Ziegler, states that it is the division between socialists and Communists that has prevented the construction of a socialist Europe. The paper concludes the interview by calling on his behalf for the creation of a 'humanist international' as a home for 'militants of the new thinking'. It will probably not be long before the USSR begins applying a social-democratic varnish to the Communist bloc in order to speed up the decay of West European political structures. With this in mind, Mrs Thatcher's reservations about a politically-integrated Europe leaning towards socialism should be taken seriously by all Western Europeans.

In the meantime, Moscow is busy promoting lobbies in favour of East–West cooperation, developing all sorts of contacts between the EEC and COMECON, and creating structures designed to institutionalise these contacts ('a mechanism and an infrastructure for direct commercial links between the EEC and COMECON')[94] and encourage pressure groups. The Supreme Soviet has been brought forward to negotiate with the Council of Europe.[95]

The Soviets are therefore resigned to West European integration and have, as always, set about making a virtue of necessity. This does not prevent their seeking to weaken Western Europe if the opportunity arises. *Pravda*[96] has quoted the judgement of F. Muhri, leader of the Austrian Communist Party, on the prospect of Austria's joining the EEC. 'Austria's entry into the EEC would signify a reinforcement of the European Community and therefore a deepening of the division of Europe.' The Soviets appear to view the European Association for Free Trade, comprising Austria and Switzerland, as a possible counterpoise to the EEC.

One more trump card must not be forgotten: Europe is not confined economically to the EEC and CAEM but also includes the European Association for Free Trade, of which the members are small and dynamically-developed states. The majority are non-aligned, with extensive commercial and economic exchanges with the EEC and the members of CAEM. The latter cooperate with the members of the European Association for Free Trade, particularly Finland and Austria but also Sweden and Switzerland, which often adapt better than the other West European countries to the interests of their partners in the East.[97]

Moscow will doubtless now begin stirring up the fears of neutral European states at the prospect of a united Europe.

The Soviets are placing most of their hopes on West Germany. The media never stint in their praise of Russo-German (and German–Soviet) cooperation, emphasising its deep historic roots. They recall that the German Tzars were always great Russian patriots; that Toukhachevsky studied in Germany; that the Germans brought skills to Russia and took on Russian nationality; that Peter the Great issued an invitation to German craftsmen to come to Russia.

We were allies in the war against Napoleon . . . the relations between our countries have always been valued by Russia. . . . [We must] understand the psychology of the Germans. For example, their painful awareness of their responsibility for the bloodshed of the War and their bitter memory of what they lost . . . today we place great hopes in our business relations with the FRG.[98]

Soviet propaganda aimed at West Germany puts the accent on 'the cultural unity of Europe', playing on the traditional German tendency to concentrate on cultural, economic and ecological, rather than political perspectives. The Soviets, advises *Literaturnaya Gazeta*, should make better use of the Russian cultural heritage in dealing with the West, casting themselves as perpetuators of Russian humanism.[99]

This type of argument is mostly directed at the West Germans, who are more prone than the French or British to gloss over the realities of Communism and Sovietisation, no doubt because of the division of Germany. To recognise the effects of Sovietisation is to have to face what separates the two Germanies. It is also in West Germany that Gorbachev's social-democratic overtures have been most successful, as they hold out the promise of political convergence and a painless solution to the German problem. The Soviets realise very well that the West German enchantment with *perestroika* is not a media show as everywhere else but the result of internal political evolution. 'The immense popularity of our *perestroika* is not a media show as everywhere else but the result of internal political evolution.'The immense popularity of our *perestroika* in West Germany is not simply fashion or groundless euphoria, but the result of a fundamental review by the citizens of the FRG of their destiny in Europe and their national interests, which are closely linked to reciprocity with Russia.' [100]

THE INTERNATIONAL COMMUNIST MOVEMENT

With *glasnost* now in force, the Soviet press is painting a worrying picture of the possibilities and prospects of the international Communist movement. In non-Communist countries 'Communists are having to face new and difficult problems on account of social-economic developments. These problems hinder their activity, the more so as the structure of the working class has become more complex.' Even worse, the 'negative phenomena' affecting socialism in practice have had disturbing consequences for the movement as a whole.[101] Soviet analysts nevertheless remain good Leninists. 'It is well known that the role of no social movement can be judged solely on the basis of quantitative criteria such as electoral influence or membership figures. The essential thing is the movement's activity and, needless to say, its results.' [102]

Communist Parties world-wide have been given essentially the same tasks as the CPSU: to take over social movements, extend widely, and practice entryism assiduously while preserving their own Leninist identity. Western European Communist Parties have been charged with approaching other leftist bodies and influencing them towards Soviet interests. 'It is important to develop an alternative Left on the Continent, which could modify the relationship of forces and trends throughout Western Europe . . . for us, to talk about European forces of the Left is to talk about . . . unity with the social-democrats, on condition that they evolve Leftwards,' Gerardo Iglesias has written.[103]

Third World Communist Parties must ally themselves with 'democratic revolutionary parties' and favour 'unions of the Left'. This strategy has been most successful in Latin America, where the

Communist movement has become an integral part of the common front of national democratic forces fighting against the expansion of imperialism and local reactionaries. The Communist Parties are particularly active in Argentina, Uruguay and Brazil. The main task of Latin-American Communists is to create broad fronts of diverse forces of whatever political orientation, in the interests of the anti-imperialist struggle which is common to them.[104]

In Equador these policies were quick to bear fruit. President Cordero, America's closest ally in Latin America, was in the spring of 1988 replaced by Rodrigo Borja, leader of the Left-wing democratic party, who after his election lost no time in renewing relations with Nicaragua, criticising his predecessor's pro-American policies and proposing approaches to the non-aligned countries, while abandoning free exchange at the same time.

The Communist Parties have put a lid on Marxism–Leninism and are now trying to compensate with pacifist rhetoric for the ideological discredit into which they had fallen. Moscow stands to gain, as appeals to the 'anti-war' aspirations of the masses increases the possibility of mobilising the population of non-Communist countries in the cause of disarmament.

Numbers of Western commentators have pronounced the international Communist movement dead. This premature optimism arises from their failure to understand the new orders from Moscow which are being executed with habitual efficiency by Communist Parties world-wide. It only takes an examination of the Communist Parties' position on defence to realise the perfect coordination of their actions with the USSR, and their continued faithful service to the ideological homeland. The Gorbachevian slogan of a denuclearised world by the year 2000 has been taken up by all the Communist Parties, including the French who had previously sided with the 'across the board' nuclear deterrence beloved of De Gaulle.

All the Communist Parties are criticising the notion of 'flexible response' and defending the concept of 'structural non-aggression' and collective security systems. All are opposed to the idea of 'Europe as a NATO prop', this having taken the place of the EDC as Moscow's *bête noire*. Communists are campaigning for the destruction of chemical weapons, an important part of the USSR's programme foir world disarmament. They have charged ahead with the Soviet slogan of liquidation of 'asymmetries' between NATO and the Warsaw Pact. NATO's aerial forces are the main target, as they are its principal source of firepower after the elimination of medium-range missiles, and its only hope of effective retaliation to an

aggressor. Every Communist Party is agitating for the establishment of
'nuclear-free zones', removal of American bases, and refusal of access to
European ports for nuclear-powered American vessels. Every Communist
Party with a seat in Parliament is demanding general reductions in military
spending, reconversion of industries with defence contracts, and relative
increase in operational spending with a corresponding decrease in procure-
ment. They are particularly opposed to any weapons requiring cooperation
and coordination within the Alliance. Thus they have attempted to block
SDI with the argument (developed by Soviet propaganda) that it is a 'new
step in the restructuring of industrial relations on the world stage'.[105] They
have likewise opposed the arms trade of their respective countries. They try
to avoid 'unilateral actions', creating instead 'broad fronts' of pacifists and
using ecological themes where possible. Even the West German Communist
Party has been congratulating itself on 'an improvement in the climate of
relations between Social-Democrats and Communists, and between Communists and Greens . . . the SDP and the Greens have taken up several of
our demands or have adopted positions similar to our own.'[106]

The general outline of Soviet strategy reveals the absolute consistency of
the Soviet positions; this strategy it also demonstrates that it does exist. Its
successes and limitations are a different matter. The European Parliament
recently voted through a resolution, introduced by a French Communist,
condemning the United States for purchasing Latin-American babies
allegedly for use in organ banks. This tale of the dismembering of children
has been spread about for some years by the Communist disinformation
machine. The vote in the European Parliament, besides being a gross insult
to our American allies, is an alarming indication of the growing Soviet
ascendancy over the Western wing of the 'common European home'. Eight
US allies are facing growing internal opposition to American nuclear
presence on their soil. New Zealand and Iceland have denied access to their
ports for nuclear-powered American vessels. The situation in Denmark
remains unstable after the fall of the government in April 1988. Similar
difficulties are already arising in the Philippines, Norway, Canada, Greece
and the Pacific. To be sure, these anti-nuclear movements reflect genuine
concerns in the population, but it would be imprudent to underestimate the
role played by Communist orchestration and propaganda in this sudden
acute outbreak of nuclear allergy. The Soviet press demonstrates that quite
clearly. *Pravda* is innocently delighted that the Faröe Islands, six years
after the creation of a Friendship Association with the USSR, have declared
themselves a 'nuclear-free zone', and that twinning with Odessa has
encouraged Vancouver to proclaim itself the first Canadian 'nuclear-free'
city.[107]

The sudden success of ecological themes in Western political circles is also
remarkable, a mere four years after the powerful Communist propaganda
machine set itself the task of replacing Western notions of a Soviet threat
with fear of an ecological apocalypse.

The Soviets have the great advantage of knowing exactly what they want. After the war, the extreme weakness of the USSR did not prevent its seizing half of Europe because it had the political willpower the West had lost. Western Europe today does not even dare to imagine a future Europe in terms other than those imposed by the Communist bloc. Fear of post-communism, skilfully fostered by Soviet propaganda, is paralysing Western leaders. It is surely time to consider what the 'common European home' could be like without communism. We would do better to offer real alternatives to the peoples under Soviet domination and help them to free themselves from their political and intellectual prison rather than simply continuing to vent therapeutic fury on a moribund regime. Gorbachevism carries a grave danger of demoralisation for the peoples of Eastern Europe, in that waiting for promised reform from above gives them an excuse to postpone the painstaking business of political recovery. The West should take care not to encourage this abdication of responsibility. Every year under communism only increases the gap between the two Europes.

NOTES

1. Speech, 25 July 1988.
2. 25 September 1988.
3. 15 June 1988.
4. No. 3, February 1988, p. 32.
5. 5 August 1988.
6. *Pravda*, 25 June 1988.
7. *Pravda*, 3 June 1988.
8. *Pravda*, 14 April 1988.
9. *Pravda*, 25 February 1988.
10. Andrei Gromyko, Budapest speech, 23 February 1988.
11. *LG*, 9 November 1988.
12. *Pravda*, 13 April 1988.
13. *Pravda*, 1 May 1988.
14. Mikhail Gorbachev, Warsaw speech, 11 July 1988.
15. *Mezdunarodnaya Zizn*, no. 4, 1988, p. 47 and no. 10, 1987, p. 10, quoted in: Gerhard Wettig, 'Friedenssicherung, Klassenkampf und Neues Denken in Gorbatschows Westpolitik', *Aussenpolitik*, IV/88.
16. *Pravda*, 28 June 1988.
17. *Moscow News,* 20 November 1988.
18. *Moscow News*, 25 July 1988.
19. A. Yakovlev in *Moscow News*, 9 October 1988.
20. *Moscow News*, 13 March 1988.
21. Speech, 1 June 1988.
22. 10 July 1987.
23. *Pravda*, 5 July 1988.
24. *International Herald Tribune*, 4 October 1988.
25. *Communist of the Armed Forces*, no. 7, April 1987, p. 86.

26. Speech to XIXth CPSU Conference.
27. *LG*, 18 May 1988.
28. *ibid.*
29. Terms used by A. Bovin, see *Pensée Russe*, 24 June 1988.
30. *LG*, 18 May 1988.
31. *ibid.*
32. *ibid.*
33. Richard Nixon, 'Dealing with Gorbachev', *New York Times* Magazine, 13 March 1988.
34. *Monde Diplomatique*, October 1987, p. 3.
35. *Pravda*, 23 October 1987.
36. *Pravda*, 9 December 1987.
37. Mikhail Gorbachev, Speech to the Plenum, 18 February 1988.
38. Mikhail Gorbachev, Speech to the XIXth CPSU Conference.
39. *RLRB*, 16 December 1987.
40. 29 October 1987.
41. *LG*, 13 July 1988.
42. See, for example, *LG*, 2 March 1988.
43. *Pravda*, 1 March 1988.
44. *LG*, 27 April 1988.
45. 10 July 1988.
46. *LG*, 6 April 1988.
47. *LG*, 17 February 1988 and *Moscow News*, 3 July 1988.
48. *RLRB*, 21 October 1988.
49. See, for example, the article by Georgy Arbatov in *Moscow News*, 25 September 1988.
50. *Pravda,* 17 February 1988.
51. *Wall Street Journal*, 7 November 1988.
52. 4 November 1987.
53. 11 August 1988.
54. Speech, 10 February 1988.
55. Speech, 8 May 1988.
56. *Moscow News*, 19 June 1988.
57. A. Yakovlev in *Moscow News*, 9 October 1988.
58. *Pravda*, 16 June 1988.
59. *LG*, 29 June 1988.
60. *Pravda*, 29 May 1988.
61. *Pravda*, 6 January 1988.
62. *Pravda*, 16 June 1988.
63. 29 July 1988.
64. *Moscow News*, 21 August 1988.
65. *Pravda*, 7 August 1988.
66. *Pravda*, 19 April 1988.
67. *Pravda*, 8 November 1987.
68. *Pravda,* 11 November 1987.
69. 5 June 1988.
70. *Moscow News*, 13 November 1988.
71. See, for example, the article by Georgy Arbatov in *Moscow News*, 25 September 1988.

72. *Moscow News*, 10 July 1988.
73. Mikhail Gorbachev, Speech to the UNO, 17 September 1987.
74. Speech to the UNO, 7 December 1988.
75. 12 June 1988.
76. *Pravda*, 23 August 1988.
77. *New York Times*, 3 December 1987.
78. *New York Times*, 2 August 1988.
79. *Communist of the Armed Forces*, no. 9, May 1988.
80. *Moscow News*, 14 August 1988.
81. *ibid.*
82. *LG*, 3 August 1988.
83. 29 March 1988.
84. *Pravda*, 6 November 1987.
85. *Pravda,* 24 April 1988.
86. 11 July 1988.
87. See, for example, the objectives of European cooperation defined by V. V. Sychev, President of COMECON, in *Pravda*, 25 June 1988.
88. 30 July 1988.
89. *LG*, 6 July 1988.
90. 25 September 1988.
91. 8 August 1988.
92. *Moscow News*, 25 September 1988.
93. 28 September 1988.
94. *Pravda*, 28 July 1988.
95. *Pravda*, 23 May 1988.
96. 20 June 1988.
97. *Moscow News*, 26 June 1988.
98. *LG*, 20 July 1988 and 14 October 1987.
99. 2 December 1987.
100. *Moscow News*, 23 October 1988.
101. *Communist of the Armed Forces*, no. 1, January 1987.
102. *Communist of the Armed Forces*, p. 10.
103. *New International Review*, no. 349, September 1987.
104. *Communist of the Armed Forces*, no. 1, January 1987, p. 12.
105. *Correspondence Armée Nation*, no. 57, March–April 1988.
106. *Unsere Zeit*, 27 January 1987.
107. 11 May 1987 and 15 September 1986.

7. *Perestroika* and the armed forces

The Western media generally present the Soviet military as the main victim of *perestroika*. The cavalier sacking of the Defence Minister and other high-ranking military officials in the wake of the Matthias Rust (the young West German pilot who landed a private plane in Red Square) affair, the resignation of Marshal Sergei Akhromeyev, Major-General of the armed forces, during Gorbachev's visit to New York in December 1988, and many increasingly transparent allusions in the military press, all serve to further this impression. However, the situation is less straightforward than it appears. *Perestroika* is affecting the Army at various levels and is as ambiguous as elsewhere.

Like the KGB, the military, being in contact with the real situation in the Soviet Union, was certainly among the first to sound the alarm that the state of affairs established under Brezhnev could not endure. The difficulties in Afghanistan could only have sharpened their realisation. There is therefore no doubt that the military wanted change and supported – if not actually inspired – the first phases of *perestroika* at least as much as the KGB. Many *perestroika* themes were appearing in the military press before they surfaced in the other media. General Louchev, Commander-in-Chief of the Warsaw Pact, was preaching 'the spirit of initiative and independence'[1] as long ago as 1983. In his book,[2] published in 1985, General Gareyev, one of the foremost military theoreticians in the USSR, criticised Stalin with a virulence not found in the civilian press until three years later. For obvious reasons, the military has consistently called for measures favouring 'scientific-technical progress', and is uneasy at the widening of the technological gap between Communist and capitalist countries. President Reagan's SDI brought these fears to a head, and probably contributed largely to the launching of *perestroika*.

The first series of Gorbachevian measures had everything to please the military. The priority given to the machine building sector (1987 'could rightly be called the year of machine building'[3]), improvement in transport, the plans for economic and scientific integration of COMECON – which was an attempted response to SDI[4] – the accent placed on industrial development of Eastern Siberia,[5] the campaign for discipline, the anti-vodka legislation, the re-launching of 'scientific-technical progress' with the creation of 'inter-sector scientific-technical complexes' designed to speed up the absorption of scientific innovations into industry – all this was an answer to the military's dreams. The Army also appreciates the necessity of Gorbachev's social programme: 'The Party's strategic line of accelerated development is not dictated solely by internal needs for development of

Soviet society, but by external circumstances and the necessity for systematic reinforcement of the defence potential of the motherland.'[6] The urgency of making the economy perform appears like a refrain running through military writings.[7]

Unfortunately for the military, *perestroika* has another side which also affects it directly. The political leadership is demanding greater results in exchange for the colossal sums allocated to the defence budget. The Army is a microcosm of Soviet society, with the same deceit, corruption, misappropriation, illegality and shoddiness. *Perestroika*, for the Army as well as the rest of society, is essentially a purge to be carried out with the help of *glasnost* and 'democratisation'. Gorbachev's ambition is to create a new, lean, mean army out of the enormous, archaically-conceived (albeit technically excellent in many areas) military machine he inherited from Brezhnev. This proposed restructuring has two complementary slogans: 'democratisation' and 'non-offensive defence'. In order to shake up the military apparatus and drag it from the complacent lethargy it enjoyed in the pre-*perestroika* period, when it felt itself immune to all criticism, the Party has authorised the media to take on the Army, leading *glasnost* into areas previously shrouded in silence. One means of frightening the military is to raise the spectre of unilateral cuts in the armed forces.

MILITARY PROBLEMS RAISED IN THE MEDIA

It would be naive to think that the Army and Navy – flesh of the people's flesh – have remained immune from all the negative and evil effects of the period of stagnation. On the contrary, the specific conditions by virtue of which practically all spheres of military activity were excluded from control and criticism by being alleged military or state secrets sometimes aggravated the situation. In two months this year, 2.5 million roubles in fines were paid for various abuses committed by Army officials. In some units a psychology of irresponsibility can be observed, with commanders and political adjuncts infringing military laws and regulations, and we note a relatively high proportion of conscripts seeking to evade service obligations (there have even been cases cited of soldiers and sergeants renting private flats); theft and vandalism are running wild; the use of soldiers and cadets for various economic purposes outside the unit detracts greatly from combat preparation. We can no longer accept the notorious bullying.[8]

This passage indicates the area of *glasnost* in the military sphere. Criticism is being directed equally at officers and the 'human raw material' placed at their disposal.

Officers
Ever since the Rust affair, the authorities have scarcely been able to find words harsh enough to berate the Army. This virulence is unprecedented in the USSR, where the military has always enjoyed a quasi-immunity to

criticism. Nowadays, comments such as 'A whole generation of our military officers has been trained to be satisfied with mediocrity'[9] have become widespread, especially after the 19th CPSU Conference.

In the eyes of the political leadership, Party organisations within the Army are largely responsible for this situation. Instead of instilling order and discipline, they are completely in thrall to the military leaders and even go so far as to take on their unwanted jobs.

> The situation in which the Secretary of the Party organisation and the other members of the elected organ are under the commander's orders and tamely carry out all his instructions is little to be recommended . . . functions must be separated – those of the Service and those of the Party. It is well known that this is not always the case.[10]
>
> At times the commander delegates his own duties to the Party organisation – such as preparing equipment and cleaning barracks.[11]

Here, as elsewhere, the question is of who has the real power; here as elsewhere, the Party has steadily lost influence, busying itself with paperwork instead of maintaining an 'informal' grip on military collectives. 'Too many officers and commanders are attempting to direct the Party organisation. And how has the Party collective reacted to all this? Unhappily, it has often resigned itself to the tone of command.'[12] The reason is that 'certain Party functionaries are afraid to criticise the military leaders.' [13]

Such is the result of the 'years of stagnation' in the military. Now, with *perestroika*, vigilance is more than ever necessary because of the new temptations on offer to weak spirits. For instance, one officer has taken six months of his troops' time to build a cooperative cafe, another has opened a garage for some private automobile speculation, a third has even used his soldiers to carry out burglaries.[14] The Party must in addition defend the oppressed by calling to order those officers who train troops 'with their fists'. It must remould the officers and correct their coarseness, brutality and arrogance, which have created an 'unhealthy atmosphere'.

Officers, however, are not only to be criticised. Their legitimate grievances are recognised. Army careers have lost much of their former prestige.[15] This is not surprising considering the conditions in which a Soviet officer lives, with crippling timetables, poor accommodation, frequent divorce, boredom and the squalid garrison existence. Ever since the 19th Party Conference, *Communist of the Armed Forces*, the monthly review which is the principal organ of the military's political leadership, has boiled over with letters from officers suffering from a crisis of vocation, over-whelmed by a feeling that their whole existence is pointless. Often the vocation of these officers was never clear in the first place. 'Unhappily, people do not always become officers by vocation. It is no secret to anyone that it is much easier to gain admission to a military academy than to university. Not because the standards are inferior, but because we are badly in need of cadets. We recruit them in the hope of filling any gaps during the process of their training,' stated General Ivan Tvetryak.[16] This can have bad consequences, to judge by frequent allusions to psychological problems among cadets. *Perestroika* in the economy only aggravates the situation. Officers have no chance to earn money by working in cooperatives. Their buying power will therefore dwindle – 'a process which has already begun' – which will erode the prestige of a military career even further.

The Ranks

Glasnost has raised the previously taboo subject of the frequently sadistic bullying of new recruits ('greens') by old hands. This is a grave problem. In 1988 30 young conscripts were, in effect, tortured to death.[18] The military press has responded as best it can by arguing that miracles cannot be expected with the standard of conscripts provided by current Soviet society. 'The illusion cannot be entertained that it is possible in one or two years to make a human being of someone with whom the family, school and Komsomol have all failed.' 'Problem' soldiers are mainly the product of inadequate parents and institutions. They have a history of brawling and vandalism, a weakness for alcohol and drugs. 'Those who suffer from overprotection are not ready for military service.' [19] In the end, all excuses fall back on the classic explanation that 'the general state of society during the years of stagnation led to the same processes affecting the armed forces.' [20]

The majority of conscripts come from vocational technical schools (PTUs)[21] where the pupils, left to themselves, fall into delinquency and alcoholism. One poll, displayed truculently by the military, showed that 37 per cent of youths had encountered bullying in the technical schools and other vocational institutions,[22] i.e. before the Army. Non-commissioned officers have been requested to remedy the situation, with particular attention to categories 'at risk':

Those from disadvantaged families; those who have often changed schools or jobs without valid reason; those with a criminal record; those susceptible to bad influences; religious believers; those who infringe discipline; drinkers; those who are lazy; those who enjoy a false prestige; those who before their military service were under the influence of idlers; those who are brutal and like to humiliate others.[23]

Essentially, the Army is confronting the same problems as the rest of society. Military discipline exists in conjunction with street law. 'In some units, particularly construction battalions, the percentage of young soldiers with anti-social backgrounds is quite considerable.'[24] Twenty per cent of conscripts are from 'problem' families.[25]

Why this sudden interest in *dedovchina* (bullying), a problem which surely did not spring up yesterday?[26] The phenomenon, explains *Moscow News*, 'is morally ignoble and militarily dangerous, as units where hatred and discord reign are more vulnerable.' [27] *Dedovchina* has lately 'taken on a nationalist hue'.[28] Once again, it is the combination of street law and nationalist passion that has impelled the authorities to act. The military press is no longer hiding the growing unease of political officials faced with an explosion of nationalism or the confusion of Army officers unable to handle the tensions. The ethnic conflicts breaking out within the USSR are reflected in the Army. The events in Karabakh aroused fierce interest and considerable *schadenfreude* in the ranks. 'For many Communists, the events themselves and the reaction they provoked among the troops came as a complete surprise.' [29] Ethnic 'microgroups' have formed within units. 'National conflicts have proliferated lately among conscripts . . . a great number of young soldiers from regions where nationalism has erupted have erroneous views and are contaminated by national egotism.'[30] 'Letters received by soldiers from their parents and friends in Azerbaijan and Armenia have sometimes explained events in a tendentious manner.'[31]

In some units 30 to 40 per cent of soldiers have poor comprehension of the Russian language, and this ignorance is on the increase.[32] Only 49 per cent of non-Russians in the USSR speak fluent Russian (24.2 per cent in Estonia, 25.4 per cent in Turkmenistan, 26.7 per cent in Georgia). Sixty per cent of non-Russian soldiers have acquired no satisfactory knowledge of Russian at secondary school.[33] In 1980 28 per cent of conscripts were from Central Asia; in 1988, it was over 37 per cent.[34]

The military press is not forthcoming on health problems in the Red Army, though the Army complains bitterly of the poor physical condition of new recruits, accusing the schools of neglecting 'basic military training', which is, in principle, obligatory for both boys and girls in the last two years of secondary school (for two hours a week). Only 2 to 3 per cent of pupils in the PTUs play a 'military-technical sport' at school.[35] For the last ten years only 20 to 25 per cent of conscripts have met the physical fitness standards laid down by the GTO.[36]

The military is beginning to find that *glasnost* is going too far. Lack of physical preparation for military service is now matched by a relaxation in ideology – sharply criticised in Army newspapers. Complaints are made of the lack of respect shown to military institutions by some '*perestroikist*' writers and journalists.[37] 'Some claim that "the Army is unnecessary" (we might as well believe that imperialism has changed its nature and become benign), that it offers nothing to the young but only makes them stupid', says *Communist of the Armed Forces*, outraged.[38] 'To affirm that military service is nothing but a waste of time and that it brings nothing to the development of personality, is the fantasy of people of diseased imagination or totally lacking in civic sentiment.' [39]

The military notes with chagrin that the two programmes of educational reform unveiled in 1988 give no place to 'basic military preparation'.[40] Also worrying is the fallout within the USSR from Soviet anti-nuclear and pacifist propaganda aimed abroad. The military certainly approves of the support given by the USSR to Western pacifists, but looks balefully on any sign of 'abstract' (i.e. without 'class' content) anti-militarism – the 'vegetarian pacifism' finding its way into the works of some Soviet authors. Pacifism is a good export product, but is unfit for domestic consumption.

The anti-war movement is developing in the world and also in our own country; people are invoking peace and disarmament more and more. The USSR and other socialist countries are at the head of this movement at state level. A broad campaign of information among the masses is necessary if we wish in these conditions to maintain our armed forces at a level sufficient to inflict a decisive response on any aggressor

states *Communist of the Armed Forces* ingenuously.[41]

The re-examination of history directed by *glasnost* is highly unpleasant to the military, which fears only 'harmful repercussions on the moral qualities of youth'.[42] 'The de-heroisation of the Great Patriotic War is a hundred times more dangerous than [Nazi Germany], as an education based on anti-heroes will produce anti-patriotism . . . the future is black for any country that educates its young generation on this basis.'[43]

A poll conducted among the two most recent intakes of conscripts revealed that 'a third of conscripts understand the danger of the arms race poorly or in a mistaken way, and dismiss the possibility of an attack by the imperialists on our country.'[44] According to another recent poll, only 47 per cent of conscripts were glad to be doing their military service.[45] In the eyes of the military, the 'informal associations' are contributing to ideological decline among the young by spreading 'foreign aesthetic values' unacceptable to socialism and the 'negativist and cynical mentality and lack of inclination for work in general and physical work in particular' so prevalent in the younger generation.[46]

Glasnost is considerably restricted with regard to the Army; many subjects, such as demography and accidents, remain taboo. But if *glasnost* contains no great revelations about the Soviet Army, it nevertheless gives indirect indications of the orientation of *perestroika* in the armed forces.

REACTIVATING THE PARTY

Ever since the 19th CPSU Conference the political leadership has been signalling the focus of its attacks on the Army. The Rust affair was only the first shot in the battle against the Brezhnevian military machine, and has been followed by a systematic attempt to reactivate the Party within the

Army. 'We have paid too dearly in the past for the fact that certain leaders escape party influence and criticism.' [47]

The first step in this reactivation is the promotion of a new generation of political officials to the highest level of the hierarchy. The *modus vivendi* more or less established during the years of stagnation between Army commanders and their political 'advisers' (in fact, political watchdogs) has been broken. An interesting article in the *Naval Review*[48] has lifted a corner of the veil laid over this subject of relations between the political and military branches of the Army. The article emphasises that a military commander's status is clear, but the same cannot be said of his political counterpart, whom the troops, 'accustomed to working in the sweat of their brow, perceive as someone superfluous'. 'There is no rule specifying when the commander must limit himself to acting on his advisers' opinion and in which cases they must take the decision together.' Often the commander turns any question remotely involving the Party over to his political adviser, thereby washing his hands of Party problems. . . . This can no longer be tolerated. Party organisation have been told to become more assertive, to end their habitual dependence on the military authorities, and to expose wrongdoing without fear of reprisal. 'Faced with inadequacy, some Communists pretend to notice nothing and adopt a *petit bourgeois* position of not getting involved, waiting for others to do so.'[49] Communist cells within the Army (one for each basic unit, i.e. one for each 100 men) have been shaken out of their purely formal existence and 'umbrella organisations' have been told to renew 'close links' with them – 'democratisation' requires it. Party organisations are no longer being judged in the Brezhnevian tradition of members recruited and wrongdoers expelled. This has caused great confusion among functionaries who had originally (in 1986) thought they could demonstrate their *perestroikist* zeal simply by increasing the number of expulsions. But the pressure has not lessened. Communists are still being ordered to shake off 'torpor' and 'formalism' and to contribute to 'shaping a correct public opinion'. 'It is inadmissible that Party activists should be so slow in inculcating into officers a creative approach to their task.'[50] This formula encapsulates the whole spirit of *perestroika*.

What means of exerting pressure do Party organisations enjoy? Every promotion of an officer depends on his *'characterisika'* – his assessment by Party officials – covering 'the moral qualities of a Communist, his response to criticism, his capacity to implement *perestroika*, his family relations, relations with his subordinates, etc.' [51] Military leaders must regularly, at Party meetings, report on their achievements.[52] The 'ray of *glasnost'* does 'not only show up inadequacy, but those concretely responsible for it'.[53] This reactivating of the Party from top to bottom heralds a major purge. The Party is providing itself with eyes and ears that will allow it to cut out the dead wood. The unilateral reduction in Red Army forces announced by Gorbachev in New York will provide an excellent pretext for this, as for every five soldiers demobilised there will be one officer discharged.[54]

BACKBONE OF THE NEW ARMY

The new Army will depend largely on officers who saw service in Afghanistan. The importance of these veterans to the Army is witnessed by a development largely unnoticed in the West: the proliferation since 1986 of 'military–patriotic clubs' run by Afghanistan veterans. *Glasnost* has remained close-mouthed about this movement, which may yet play a decisive role in the evolution of the USSR. The few snippets of information that can be gathered here and there form only a partial scenario.

The movement originated with, on one side, the Afghanistan veterans, adjusting badly to civilian life, badly regarded by the population, and facing indifference and even hostility from local authorities. On the other side were adolescents and youths from the technical schools, borstals and orphanages, eager to hear about the wartime exploits of their elders. The veterans suggested sharing their martial science with their young disciples. Halls were procured, equipment found where possible, and the clubs took shape. To go by press accounts, local authorities were slow to encourage these initiatives. Neither the state nor the economic enterprises were willing to finance them.[55] But the political leadership was quick to see the profit to be gained from the clubs. They would be a way of keeping veterans occupied, a 'service for order' in the technical schools and a means of talent-spotting for the commandos and MVD special forces. They would also help to 'de-bureaucratise' the Komsomol. The military–patriotic education dispensed by the Komsomol before and immediately after military service had become a pure formality and was characterised by 'a gap between the ideological and political–moral preparation and the military and military–technical preparation of youth for the defence of the motherland'.[56] The latter was being neglected in favour of the former. The military welcomed the appearance of these veteran-inspired clubs:

We suffer from a drastic lack of cadres capable of inculcating in the young the basics indispensable for service in the armed forces, of educating them in the heroic traditions of the past . . . veterans of the Great Patriotic War had played an inestimable role in the accomplishment of this task. But unfortunately their number is diminishing each year. Now it is the young reservists who help to do this work, and above all those who have known the difficult proof of war, notably in fulfilling their internationalist duty in Afghanistan. A large number of them have decided of their own initiative to contribute to the cause of military–patriotic education, by creating associations of all sorts, which adolescents are eager to join. However, state organs have long been unaware of the activities of these internationalist soldiers. They have not received the indispensable help and support of the Komsomol. In 1987 the Komsomol Central Committee attempted to reverse the negative tendency in this area, to make better use of the strengths of this category of reservist. As the system of military–patriotic education dependent on the state suffers from considerable inadequacies, resources must be found enabling this to be remedied.[57]

The gorkoms (city Party committees) have created 'military–patriotic sections' for themselves. There has been an upsurge of 'Soviets of veterans' which oversee the various clubs.[58] If the Komsomol (which itself runs many military–patriotic clubs) is showing some reservations towards a movement not in its control, the directors and staff of the technical schools seem overjoyed by this unexpected development, which can only ease their load. Military–patriotic club members are keeping order in the dormitories so well that they have been invited by local police to assist in maintaining municipal order.[59] Among club members

could be founded rockers, punks and headbangers . . . but they have changed . . . adolescents joining the clubs straight from 'street school' . . . who have had confrontations with the police and a history of neighbourhood 'exploits' . . . many were considered irredeemable. But after some months the young people had acquired a new moral foundation.[60]

The regime hopes that in getting a grip on the military–patriotic clubs, Komsomol will be able to channel their energy into economically useful jobs.

The clubs may become active and able collaborators with the Komsomol in the task of forming a wider range of interests among young people of military service age, and later in the reserves. They can help with their integration at the factory, encourage them to master a technical skill, or cultivate an individual allotment, through the collectives of the Komsomol.[61]

The military–patriotic clubs are turning out parachutists and other commandos, 'red Rambos', in the words of one *samizdat* publication.[62] In Central Asia, they also help with Russification propaganda.[63]

It is impossible to gain any precise knowledge of the extent of the phenomenon. The total number of clubs and members is unknown. In Siberia the oldest club, founded in 1981, has 500 members, divided according to their chosen service field, from submarinists to assault units.[64] Another club, cited in *Communist of the Armed Forces*,[65] each year prepares 50 young people for entry into military academies. In the Krasnoyarsk region, there are 27 of these clubs.[66] The February 1988 Congress for leaders of Siberian military–patriotic clubs registered more than 100 people. A similar congress in Novorosisk in August 1988 assembled more than 2,500 club officers, this time from all over the USSR. An association of military–patriotic clubs was formed on that occasion.[67] The congress adopted a resolution calling for nationwide development of the movement and for closer collaboration with state bodies responsible for preparing the young for military service.[68] In February 1988 a CPSU decree made the clubs' existence official.[69] Permanent bodies to coordinate the clubs have been set up at *obkom* level. However, official reservations still persist with regard to these 'irregulars', as a commentary in the *Military*

Historical Review attests:[70] 'It is difficult to agree with the allegations of certain functionaries in these circles who claim an exclusive role in the preparation of youth for military service, setting their activity in opposition to State military–patriotic education.'

It is frightening to imagine the consequences if this movement grows: young delinquents taken in hand by frustrated fanatics are the basis of these nurseries for a budding Soviet 'special force' that seem to be spreading through the country like a burning powder trail. The day the CPSU decides to change from the carrot to the stick, it will have no trouble recruiting 'special forces' to crush popular uprisings. And if it is decided to bring the benefits of 'internationalist aid' to other peoples, the means will be to hand.

NATIONALIST POLICIES WITHIN THE ARMY

The Party is urging the military to show greater boldness and initiative in the area of inter-ethnic relations so as to make the Army a true 'school of internationalism'. 'Indigenisation' of the officer corps has been recommended: 'There are too few officers of Central Asian origin. Young people from Central Asia, Transcaucasia and the Baltic states must be selected for entry into the military academies. Military and Party leaders must include representatives of these nationalities.'[71] 'It is well known that the number of students in the military academies from the Central Asian republics and Transcaucasia does not correspond to their proportion of the total production of the USSR.'[72] Commissions specialising in inter-ethnic relations have been created under the auspices of Party organs and charged with spreading the 'positive experience' gained in this area and analysing the difficulties encountered.

The specialised press is echoing these recommendations: 'avoid excessive concentrations of conscripts of the same nationality . . . [and] distribute soldiers of different origins equally',[73] and if you cannot prevent the formation of 'national micro-groups' which have 'proliferated recently after the events in Karabakh', take care to prevent the emergence of any leader; if this happens, act quickly 'during the period when the new recruits are adapting to the military collective'.[74] Squad leaders must be chosen from the predominant nationality.[75] Above all, national habits must be eradicated as 'it has no right to exist unless it is one of the factors contributing to the defence capacity of our country.'[76] No detail must be overlooked as insignificant in the area of nationalism: 'The officer must be aware of moments when questions seeming to pertain to daily life take on a nationalistic colouration . . . some leaders refuse to recognise this in their educational practice. But I am convinced that the demographic situation will force them to take decisive measures in this respect.'[77]

Intensive special Russian courses are being recommended, following the example of the American Navy where 'most blacks, Puerto Ricans and Asiatics speak better English than, for example, Uzbeks, Turkmenis and Azeris speak Russian.'[78]

MOVING ON TO 'QUALITATIVE PARAMETERS'

At present *perestroika* within the armed forces is mostly taking the form of a campaign for discipline [one of the military's 'gravest problems' is the 'education' of personnel[79]] and against waste and corruption. The Army has been requested to emphasise 'qualitative parameters', to 'eradicate its self-satisfaction, incompetence, laziness and negligence', to 'perfect the top ranks'[80] and 'improve the training of NCOs'.[81] 'Democratisation' occupies a central place in this scheme. 'We must know how to use democratic organisations in the interests of improved combat capability.' [82]

Effective 'counter-propaganda' aimed at reviving troop morale also comes into it. 'Today we cannot expose the ideological twists of imperialism simply by informing soldiers of the disquieting events taking place in the world. We are trying to inculcate more effectively a hatred of the enemies of the Motherland, peace and progress.' [83] Parity in armaments may be grudgingly accepted, 'but in the spiritual sphere, the moral-political qualities of Soviet citizens, of the personnel of the Army and Navy, we have incontestable advantages and are continuing to reinforce them, and to maintain our ideological superiority, which represents an important strategic factor.' [84]

RESTRUCTURING OF THE ARMED FORCES AND THE POLITICAL LINE

In the military sphere, too, Gorbachev has brought to a fine art the making of virtues out of necessities. For obvious economic and demographic reasons the 'extensive' development of the armed forces had to come to a halt, and the military made to give more value for money. He saw how to extract maximum political advantage from this painful transition and the way things are going it is even possible that the 'correlation of forces' may be shifting in favour of the USSR as a result of the disarmament proceedings so skilfully set in train by General Secretary Gorbachev. Changes required by the reconfiguration of Soviet forces are being cleverly disguised as arms control measures, aimed above all at breaking down the cohesion of the Atlantic Alliance. Alexander Zinoviev's quip comes to mind: The USSR is prepared to reduce its armed forces by half, on condition that this doubles its military potential.

The priority assigned to 'qualitative parameters' is today prompting the USSR to an army reduced in numbers [a part of the reduction in strength may be transferred to the MVD forces, as happened in China], but more professional, with less, but better-performing equipment. The elimination of marginal armaments, presented as a unilateral reduction, has had an immense political payoff. The evolution of weaponry – particularly conventional weaponry – and the rapid improvement in its technology must soon bring about a change in the command structure of the main units of the land armies, aimed at greater efficiency of command and coordination of firepower, while cutting back on manpower. The accent is on improving the 'human factor': 'Let us not forget what Lenin said: "As much as modern technology, modern warfare demands high quality human material." '[85]

If limited to that, the restructuring heralded by Soviet propaganda and the unilateral reduction offered by Gorbachev in New York in December 1988 will not affect the Warsaw Pact's offensive capacity, which has increased dramatically since 1970. The evolution that has taken place in operations, organisation and equipment of the land and air forces and in the operational system of command shows that the Soviets have provided themselves with the means to wage a conventional war in Europe.[86] In the last ten years the United States has produced 7,600 tanks, the USSR 25,300; the United States has produced 3,200 pieces of artillery, the USSR 27,300; the ratio of multiple rocket launchers produced over the same period is 17 : 1 in favour of the USSR.[87] During the first four years of *perestroika*, the number of tanks, planes, missiles, etc., produced by Soviet factories has remained unchanged at several times higher than the American figure despite all the rhetoric about the 'reconversion' of military industries to civilian use, so beloved for some time now by Soviet propaganda.

Nuclear deterrence is the sole obstacle preventing the Soviets from putting their immense advantage to military or political use. *Pravda*[88] has summed up the situation thus: 'In the age of nuclear weapons, there is no chance of attaining world domination.' The classic argument advanced by Soviet propaganda must give pause for though by its very formulation: 'In a nuclear war there could be no victor: that is why it is indispensable to seek the means of finally liquidating nuclear weapons.'[89] In other words, the accumulation of nuclear weapons has made war impossible. As General Louchev has written:

The arms race has reached its apogee, when nuclear weapons cannot be employed, at the present hour or in the future, to attain reasonable political goals. . . . In these conditions we cannot assure security but by lowering the level of armed confrontation, by decreasing and finally eliminating totally, nuclear weapons and other weapons of mass destruction.[90]

'Technical progress in the military sphere has restricted the possibilities for direct use of many types of weapons in armed confrontation. Thus the negative effects of the imperialist policy of the arms race is increased.[91] Nuclear arms, more than anything else, are seen by Soviet theoreticians as a foul played by history against the progressive forces of the world: 'In a nuclear war, the disparity between the expected and the actual results becomes unpredictable . . . when it becomes nuclear, war ceases to be a factor for social change [i.e. for imposing Communist regimes] or a means of resolving the contradictions of internal or international life.' [92] The existence of nuclear arms hinders and obstructs the revolutionary movement, required now not to provoke imperialism too openly for fear of nuclear retaliation. 'The nuclear age demands extreme prudence from revolutionary forces in the choice of forms of struggle.'[93]

The programme which Gorbachev launched on 15 January 1986 with his proposals for the total liquidation of nuclear weapons fits with perfect logic into this analysis, as does the Euromissile treaty ratified in 1988. The USSR is ready to sacrifice a part of its nuclear arsenal, neutralised to a large extent by that of the United States, in exchange for substantial military and political advantages. True, the INF Treaty has required the Soviets to destroy twice as many missiles as the Americans but it has removed the main NATO weapon the Soviets really feared; in addition, it has accelerated the dynamic of disarmament in Europe so that 'partial victory' (a term which reappeared in Soviet military writings in 1985) that is, victory in the European theatre, again becomes possible. The INF Accord is 'the link by which we can hope to pull out the entire chain of problems of nuclear disarmament.'[94] The military cannot but be pleased at this evolution and the prospect offered by arms control, which has halted American technological advances at the very moment when they could have widened the gap between the two camps. This will give the USSR the time to make up for the ground it has lost in any particular field (with the help of espionage facilitated by _détente_).

Adopting the doctrinal principles of 'non-offensive defence' and 'reasonable sufficiency' has the obvious advantage of making the Americans and their allies responsible for the arms race: 'The limits of reasonable sufficiency in the military potential of the USSR and Warsaw Pact countries depends on the position and actions of NATO and the United States.'[95] If the Soviets manage to put this line of propaganda over on the West, governments will have increasing difficulty in persuading public opinion to approve allocations to the military budget; and at a time when the Americans would like to see the Europeans contribute more to their own defence, such conflicts could split the Atlantic Alliance. Time will tell whether these principles amount to more than a simple slogan inspired by the 'war of diplomacy', of which the Soviet military was the first to see the importance. In the meantime, the _Military Historical Review_ is aptly quoting Lenin's remark that 'it is indispensable to prepare the cadres of the proletariat for offensive military action.'[96]

From a strictly military viewpoint, Soviet military leaders cannot but approve of the arms control measures achieved up to this point. However, increasingly thinly-veiled criticisms of the political leadership are appearing in the military press. If high-level military leadership is adopting, more or less, the 'politicals' line, the analyses and commentaries appearing in the military press – including the political organ of the military – nevertheless often flagrantly contradict the official words.

It may be that 'theoretical' disagreements are not simply the grumbling caused by the arrival of *perestroika* in the military. Having enjoyed a quiet life under Brezhnev, the military cadres are now being assailed by all sorts of contradictory demands, such as reinforcing discipline while developing democracy in the ranks. The politicals are spoiling for a quarrel with them, having themselves been shaken from their pleasant lethargy by the reactivated Party base, ordered by recent directives to be critical of its leaders. Of course, there are methods of self-defence, for example, engaging in prophylatic self-criticism which costs nothing. But all this agitation cannot but be disagreeable, added to which is the insolence of journalists, emboldened by *glasnost*, making fun of the military's spelling mistakes and casting doubt on the usefulness of military service to the young. The military must indeed be longing for the happy days of stagnation. Even worse, the nightmare of unilateral reduction in the armed forces, similar to that effected by Khrushchev from 'which we are still suffering',[97] is returning to haunt the military. In July 1988 in Washington Marshal Akhromeyev had explicitly stated that there could be no question of unilateral reductions. The military are quoting Lenin's dictum that: 'Only after having disarmed the bourgeoisie can the proletariat lay down its arms, all the while remaining faithful to its historic world mission.' [98] Added to this is another complaint: the 'lax' policy towards nationalities, which is provoking increasing exasperation among the military. *Red Star* is following developments in the Baltic states very closely, and is continually attacking the Party's 'passivity' in the face of nationalist excesses. *Military Historical Review* has been displaying a startlingly virulent national-bolshevism since January 1989. A February 1989 editorial significantly recalled that it was the Polish army which in 1981 saved Poland from chaos.

None of these grievances can be expressed plainly. Who would risk criticising 'democratisation', *glasnost* in the Army, and so forth?

On the other hand, over more technical and ideological developments the military express their feelings to their hearts' content. They remind malignantly that Stalin let Hitler take him by surprise, having 'overestimated political means' at the expense of 'military means'. 'Lack of cohesion between political and military measures . . . and above all the under-estimation of military means, can inflict considerable damage on the cause of defending the conquests of socialism.' [99] Just when the 'new thinking' is preaching 'de-ideologicisation of international relations', numerous recent studies, including some published in 1986–7 under the direction of the Institute of Military History, are saying things like:

The present stage of development of mankind is characterised by a confrontation, without precedent in its intensity and acuity, between two ideologies: Communist and bourgeois.[100]

The whole world has become the arena for the struggle between the social systems. The struggle between the two systems is the axis around which the domestic and international life of all states of every type is turning.[101]

It is a global contradiction on a world scale. It is present in all countries, all regions, all spheres of social life. All the political processes and the events taking place in the world are linked to this fundamental contradiction, many follow from it.[102]

With regard to peace, military writers are saying: 'Communists have never been and never can be pacifists.' [103] 'The struggle for peace has an anti-imperialist character . . . socialism and peace are indissoluble.'[104] Their opinion of war is that 'In judging war, class is a determining criterion, it overrides all other considerations, including moral and judicial ones.'[105] The military is not forgetting that most of the advances of the international Communist movement have been due to wars: 'an extremely important consequence of the Second World War was a radical modification of global progressive forces . . . the world socialist system was put in place . . . the Communist movement was strengthened enormously in the capitalist countries.'[106] Naturally 'a victory for the revolution is perfectly possible in conditions of peaceful co-existence . . . history has not revealed a direct link between wars and revolutions but there has been and remains, a certain coincidence',[107] 'a dialectical link'. 'It is enough to say that in certain conditions war can accelerate the maturation of objective and subjective conditions for revolution and even facilitate its victory . . . war increases social tensions and aggravates class contradictions.' [108]

It is nuclear weapons, as always, that have upset the 'dialectical link' between war and revolution. 'Is it imaginable to arrive at the world victory of the revolution by means of nuclear war?' The Soviets are thus reduced to waiting for 'the objective conditions for revolution to come to maturity' [109] within countries, and to making pronouncements such as

always, at every instant, the Soviet soldier is ready to lend a helping hand to fraternal peoples of socialist countries fighting for their national liberation. The Vietnamese and the Egyptian fellah, the Ethiopian revolutionaries and the Indian builders from the metallurgical combine at Bilhai, the Nicaraguan and Afghan workers have experienced the effective class solidarity shown by the Soviets.[110]

This appeared at the time when official propaganda was trying to convince the non-Communist world that the USSR had been regretting its Third World adventures and had renounced the Brezhnev doctrine.

In more technical areas, particularly nuclear deployment, the gap between political and military thinking is just as wide. The military is evidently annoyed by the rhetoric about the world-wide threat to mankind posed by the 'nuclear catastrophe' and by the tendency to present nuclear war as some sort of natural disaster, 'non-historical and outside class relations'.

Nuclear war cannot be a means of attaining political goals. Today, this is an axiom. But nuclear war is still war, brought about by politics and nothing else, it is the continuation of the politics that precedes it. . . . War, including nuclear war, is prepared and let loose by concrete social forces . . . we consider the distinction between 'conventional war' and 'nuclear catastrophe' in modern warfare as highly problematic. . . . The development of conventional weapons is such that they can be compared, from the point of view of effectiveness, to weaker and less efficient nuclear weapons . . . when low-power nuclear weapons are employed, war remains linked to politics [i.e. political objectives can be pursued through the armed struggle].[111]

The article concludes with the acid remark that: 'The more competent the specialist, the more he is inclined to ask himself questions . . . and it would be right to say that no one can claim to know the truth in the last instance when faced with the problem of the links between nuclear war and politics.'

Some military studies openly mention the possibility of using nuclear weapons in Europe to dissuade the European nations from aligning themselves with the United States in case of conflict. In a Third World War,

it could be supposed that the capitalist countries will not all play an equal part . . . many will be fearful of the consequences of war . . . the repartition of political-military forces will not remain identical throughout the war . . . a change in the political position of states, in modern warfare, could be induced by nuclear strikes on administrative and economic centres . . . the fear of incurring nuclear strikes may dissuade certain capitalist countries from entering into war . . . certain capitalist countries trying to throw off United States' influence and establish an independent policy, a policy of non-participation in a nuclear war.[112]
A nuclear strike could, in a brief period, totally change the situation, the relationship of forces.[113]

This theme was revived in 1988: 'With surprise use of nuclear weapons, the aggressor has the possibility of attaining from the first those results which can have a decisive influence on the course and even the outcome of the war.'[114] 'In current conditions, the presence of nuclear weapons offers the aggressor great possibilities for massive surprise strikes . . . in order to take the strategic initiative and inflict immense losses on the victim which could determine the outcome of the war in favour of the aggressor.' [115]

It may well be that the need to economise and the military's loss of confidence in the 'human factor' after the defeat in Afghanistan have led Soviet strategists to regard nuclear weapons in a new light. They would be much less burdensome than conventional arms and could give the Soviet Union a power disproportionate to its current economic and human resources. In a Europe divorced from the United States, deprived of an American deterrent, nuclear weapons could be the very instrument – at once political and military – long awaited by Soviet strategy. Moscow's recent winning-over to 'minimal deterrence', in contrast to its previous sensational declarations on the 'de-nuclearisation of the planet by the year 2000' perhaps lies in just such a new analysis of the 'correlation of forces'.

The scale of the tug-of-war between the political leadership and the military should not be exaggerated, particularly in the theoretical department. The Army's internal *perestroika* is certainly arousing fierce resentment. But the above-mentioned analyses are not contrary to the 'new thinking': just the opposite. For internal use, the accent is differently placed, but the main principles of Gorbachevian foreign policy and their immediate application are clearly outlined. Two elements contributed to CPSU policy: the KGB and the military. The first concentrates on propaganda for use abroad, manipulation of Western opinion, and involvement of the capitalist nations in maintaining the Communist order. Adherents to this line are ready to make relatively extensive concessions, such as the introduction of *glasnost*, in order to obtain Western aid. The military, also aware of the need for Western funds, technology and disarmament, is uneasy at the repercussions within the USSR from pacifist and anti-nuclear propaganda. Less externally-oriented, they fear that the political leadership will let go the bird in hand, and that no advantage from the West can compensate for the harm done by making ideological and other concessions too lightly. The economic crisis has for the moment strengthened the position of the first side, and cannot but aggravate the tensions between it and the military, with the Army threatened with cutbacks. However, these disagreements are about tactics, not strategy. Communist policy has always combined seduction with intimidation. It is quite natural that there should be disputes on the relative amount to be added of these two basic ingredients of Leninism.

NOTES

1. *RLRB*, 28 October 1987.
2. M. A. Gareyev, M. V. Frounze, *Military Theoretician*, Moscow, 1985.
3. *Military Messenger*, no. 11, 1987, p. 30.
4. See *Military Historical Review*, no. 7, 1986, and *Communist of the Armed Forces* (*CAF*), no. 9, May 1987, p. 30.
5. See *Military Historical Review*, no. 4, April 1986.
6. *CAF*, no. 22, November 1986, p. 85.
7. 'The creation of a new generation of aeroplanes, nuclear submarines and other modern military technical systems not only requires scientific research. . . . A strong economy is necessary, capable of producing micro-processors and other computer elements' (*CAF*, no. 21, Nov. 86, p. 10). 'By realising the Party programme, we are ensuring that the imperialists will not overtake us in any military domain' (*CAF*, no. 22, November 1986, p. 25).
8. *Pravda*, 10 April 1988.
9. *CAF*, no. 17, September 1988. 'We must face the truth: some of us have lost the sense of duty and responsibility necessary to accomplish their obligations and tasks,' declared General Yazov, Minister of Defence, in *Red Star* on 18 July 1987. Elsewhere it has been written that 'some commanders are preoccu-

pied with creating superficial order, refusing to "wash dirty linen in public" '
(*CAF*, no. 5, March 1988, p. 4).

10. *CAF*, no. 16, August 1988.
11. *CAF*, no. 21, November 1988.
12. *CAF*, no. 17, September 1988, p. 21.
13. *CAF*, no. 19, October 1988, p. 27.
14. *CAF*, no. 20, October 1988; no. 10, May 1987 and no. 22, November 1988.
15. *CAF*, no. 18, September 1988, p. 68.
16. *Moscow News*, 21 February 1988. General Tretiak is Vice-Minister of Defence, Commander-in-Chief of the Aerial Defence Forces.
17. *CAF*, no. 22, November 1988, p. 31.
18. *RLRB*, 19 October 1988. Most of the victims were Caucasian.
19. *CAF*, no. 2, January 1988, p. 70. General Tretiak says the same: 'It is not the army which is responsible [for bullying]. It is the consequence of the education received by the young in their own environment. I can assure you that before the 1960s there was no violence within the Army.'
20. *CAF*, no. 4, February 1988, p. 16.
21. *CAF*, no. 21, November 1988, p. 79.
22. *CAF*, no. 4, February 1988, p. 19.
23. *CAF*, no. 4, February, 1988, pp. 78-9.
24. *CAF*, no. 5, March 1988, p. 41. Construction battalions are 'dumping units', non-combatant, with many Central Asian and Caucasian conscripts.
25. *CAF*, no. 4, February 1988, p. 20.
26. A hypothesis mentioned by Yuri Poliakov suggests that *dedovchina* dates from 1967, the year in which military service was decreased from three to two years. The 'old hands' were so resentful of the fortunate new intake that they decided to make them pay in the first year. The tradition was then passed down from generation to generation.
27. 20 November 1988.
28. *CAF*, no. 21, November 1988.
29. *CAF*, no. 20, October 1988.
30. *CAF*, no. 16, August 1988.
31. *CAF*, no. 22, November 1988, p. 57.
32. *CAF*, no. 24, December 1987, p. 40.
33. *Military Messenger*, no. 12, 1988, p. 12.
34. *RLRB*, 14 September 1988.
35. *RLRB*, no. 4, February 1988, p. 23.
36. *CAF*, no. 23, December 1988, p. 24. 'GTO' stands for 'Prepared for Labour and Defence'. General Tretiak remarked in his interview with *Moscow News*: 'The level of physical development of some youths does not meet the standards required for military service.'
37. 'Driven by a thirst for sensation, journalists are showing a tendentious attitude, a lack of respect towards military officers in general' (*Military Messenger*, no. 9, 1988, p. 5).
38. No. 15, August 1988.
39. *CAF*, no. 2, January 1988, p. 25.
40. *CAF*, no. 23, December 1988, p. 23.
41. No. 20, October 1988, p. 38. 'Abstract ideas of pacifism are spreading in the pages of certain of our publications, which harms the cause of armed defence of

our Motherland, and blunts the feeling of political vigilance in some Soviet citizens. . . . This kind of article does nothing but oil the wheels of our class enemy. . . . We must never forget that love for the Motherland is indissociable from hatred of her enemies, whatever the "partisans of pseudo-humanism" might say' (*CAF*, no. 2, January 1988, p. 12).

42. *CAF*, no. 4, February 1988, p. 13.
43. *Military Historical Review*, no. 9, 1988, p. 25.
44. *Military Messenger*, no. 2, 1988, p. 44.
45. *CAF*, no. 23, December 1988, p. 24.
46. *CAF*, no. 24, December 1987, p. 69.
47. *Naval Review*, no. 11, 1988, p. 10.
48. No. 8, 1988, pp. 50–3.
49. *CAF*, no. 22, November 1988, p. 5.
50. *Naval Review*, no. 5, 1988, p. 10.
51. *Military Messenger*, no. 4, 1988, p. 8. Most officers are CPSU members. By virtue of the principle of 'unity of command', their function is military and political at the same time.
52. *Naval Review*, no. 11, 1988, pp. 9–10.
53. *CAF*, no. 20, October 1988, p. 13.
54. *Moscow News*, 18 December 1988.
55. *Pravda*, 24 September 1987.
56. *CAF*, no. 20, October 1988, p. 13.
57. *CAF*, no. 4, February 1988, pp. 22–3.
58. *ibid.*, p. 24.
59. *CAF*, no. 21, November 1988, pp. 77–8.
60. *ibid.*, p. 80.
61. *CAF*, no. 7, April 1988, p. 73.
62. See *Pravda*, 12 August 1988.
63. *RLRB*, 24 May 1988.
64. *Pravda*, 12 August 1988.
65. No. 4, February 1988.
66. *RLRB*, 19 September 1988.
67. *Pravda*, 11 and 15 August, 1988.
68. *CAF*, no. 20, October 1988, p. 13.
69. *Pravda*, 12 August 1988.
70. No. 5, 1988, pp. 77–8.
71. *CAF*, no. 21, November 1988.
72. *Naval Review*, no. 11, 1988, p. 44.
73. *Naval Review*, no. 16, August 1988.
74. *Naval Review*, no. 17, September 1988, p. 37; *Military Messenger*, no. 10, 1988, p. 16; *Naval Review*, no. 10, 1988, p. 52.
75. *Naval Review*, no. 11, June 1988.
76. *Naval Review*, no. 2, January 1988, p. 14.
77. *Naval Review*, no. 11, 1988, p. 41.
78. *ibid.*, p. 44.
79. *CAF*, no. 23, December 1988, p. 16.
80. *Military Messenger*, no. 2, 1988, pp. 18–19.
81. *Military Messenger*, no. 8, 1988, p. 5.
82. *Military Historical Review*, no. 3, 1988, p. 10.

83. *ibid.*, p. 7.
84. *CAF*, no. 20, October 1988, p. 38.
85. *CAF*, no. 23, 1988, p. 25.
86. See Georges Tan Eng Bok, 'Soviet military strength, European security and long-term deterrence', Centre de sociologie de la défense nationale, September 1988.
87. See Angello Codevilla, 'Is there still a Soviet threat?', *Commentary*, November 1988, pp. 23-8.
88. 30 January 1988.
89. *Military Historical Revue*, no. 9, 1988, p. 76.
90. *Military Historical Revue*, no. 6, 1987, pp. 3-4.
91. *CAF*, no. 12, 1987, p. 91.
92. S. A. Tiuchevitch, 'War and the contemporary world', Moscow, 1986, p. 7.
93. *CAF*, no. 7, April 1987, p. 86.
94. *CAF*, no. 22, November 1987, p. 94.
95. *CAF*, no. 12, June 1988, p. 44.
96. *Military Historical Review*, No. 4, 1988, p. 20.
97. Interview with General Tretiak in *Moscow News*.
98. *CAF*, no. 10, May 1987, p. 21.
99. *CAF*, no. 18, September 1987, p. 12.
100. Y. Y. Kirchin, V. M. Popov, R. A. Savuchkin, 'The political content of contemporary wars', Moscow 1987, p. 8.
101. *ibid.*, p. 249.
102. *ibid.*, p. 255.
103. Tiuchkevitch, 1986, p. 203.
104. *ibid.*, p. 210.
105. A. S. Milovidov, 'The military-theoretical heritage of V. I. Lenin and the problems of contemporary war', Moscow 1987, p. 8.
106. Kirchin, 1987, p. 243.
107. Tiuchkevitch, 1986, pp. 86-7.
108. *Military Historical Review*, no. 10, 1987, p. 4.
109. *ibid.*, pp. 6-7.
110. *CAF*, no. 16 August 1988, p. 81.
111. *CAF*, no. 21, November 1988.
112. Kirchin, 1987, pp. 259-70.
113. *CAF*, no. 19, September 1987, p. 24.
114. M. M. Kirian in *Military Historical Review*, no. 6, 1988, p. 17.
115. *Military Historical Review*, no. 9, 1988, p. 72.

Conclusion

Only history can judge a figure and his time; but though the Gorbachev chapter is far from closed, it may not be too soon to venture some observations.

The most striking of many contrasts is between *perestroika* within the USSR, which is only skimming the surface, and the spectacular successes of Soviet diplomacy abroad. This goes to the root of Leninism, which runs well only when there is something to destroy. In a ruined world, like the USSR in 1921 and even more so today, LKeninism is forced to go against its nihilist grain. It must restrain itself in order to let the material base necessary for survival regenerate. It chafes at this enforced self-limitation. As the experience of *perestroika* has shown, as soon as society recovers a little, begins to advance political demands and form independent economic organisations, brute Leninism returns at full speed. The troops crushing Georgian demonstrators are there not to prevent inter-ethnic massacres, but to smash a genuine democratic movement trying to put Gorbachevian slogans into practice. The cooperative movement had scarcely gathered steam when repressive legislation was brought to bear on it.

Abroad, the problems have not been so thorny. There, the way open for subversion of anything but 'socialism' is broad and inviting, and Leninist strategy – refined to perfection – is doing great things. The discretion and camouflage which the Party is obliged to apply at home have proven more profitable abroad. Forced by domestic crises to learn subtlety, the Party is turning this newfound knowledge to good advantage in diplomacy.

Ideology remains a key factor to the Soviet regime, though these days the Leninist stamp has all but obliterated the Marxist original. Like Jaruzelski, Gorbachev thinks in terms of power while invoking the public good. So far, he has managed to make the crises an instrument with which to increase his personal power and eliminate potential rivals. He has used the amulet of *glasnost* to transform the current woeful condition of the Soviet Union into a lever for the Party, 'the initiator of *perestroika*'. He has used the crimes of communism to give a second wind to the regime guilty of them. He has channelled the legitimate desire of the Soviet peoples for an end to slavery into restoring the Party's power, which was beginning to wear out. He is blackmailing the Soviet peoples and the international community by claiming that the failure of *perestroika* would be a disaster for mankind. In fact, the real disaster would be for the CPSU. The regime's hijacking and cynical exploitation of the unanimous desire for change to a 'normal' life is its supreme insult to the subject populations. The Party is systematically sowing confusion in order to prevent lucid thought and strength of will . . .

among its opponents. Sovspeak under Brezhnev was, all in all, less deceptive, or less profoundly so, than the current '*perestroikist*' line. It used at least to show up the nature of the regime which produced it. Nowadays the Communist regime pretends to be the opposite of what it is. The Party, by drawing attention to past massacres, is distracting it from the fact that terror is not the regime's only or even its chief weapon. Lies are much more important. These days, terror is decreasing while hypocrisy is on the increase.

What will be the outcome of the current chain of events? It is difficult to tell without being able, in the present turmoil, to separate the grain of future developments from the chaff. Even in studying the past, analysis of causes is far from easy. So what can possibly be said about things taking place today, beyond noting certain trends and factors which appear likely to affect the future evolution of the Soviet peoples?

Since Gorbachev's elimination of the 'conservatives' at the end of September 1988, the regime seems to be tightening the screws again, moving towards increased repression and shelving economic reform. The proposed publication of Solzhenitsyn in *Novy Mir* was cancelled in October 1988; the Karabakh Committee was arrested and the Democratic Union harassed in December; the Decree of 29 December 1988 forbade cooperatives to engage in any activity even remotely political or intellectual (particularly publishing and teaching); the Decree of 5 January 1989 gave preferential treatment to cooperatives charging state-fixed prices, with the purpose of protecting society from the social, ideological and moral danger represented by the co-operatives';[1] the Kharkov Cogress, devoted to agriculture, saw the return in force of Brezhnevian sovspeak (the solution to supply problems depends on 'the activity of Party organisations'), echoed by Gorbachev in his praise of the kolkhoz system; price reform has been abandoned; and a resolution entitled 'Opposition to attempts to create political structures hostile to the CPSU' was promulgated in February 1989 and implemented by a series of repressive measures against the Popular Fronts. The *ukase* of 8 April 1989, of which Article 11(1) laid down periods of detention of up to three years and fines of up to 2,000 roubles for 'attempts to discredit state organs and social organisations', has tightened legislation in force under Brezhnev.

All these actions form too clear a picture to argue that they represent merely random impulses. Time will tell whether they are a simple backlash or the beginning of a new sustained CPSU offensive against Soviet society. For the Soviet opposition, remaining doubts were dispelled after the April 1989 events in Georgia. The first communiqué of the 'Liberty and Democracy' movement, created after the *ukase* of 8 April and the military intervention in Georgia, states:

The new thaw has ended. We have returned to Terror, not stagnation. The laws adopted these last months have no parallel except with Stalinist laws. And they are nothing to the tanks crushing people, the killings in the streets, and the regiments of murderers armed with sharpened spades.

Grigoriantz declared on the same occasion: 'The regime has only to throw the rest of the world off the scent and maintain the illusion for the next few months' (*Pensée Russe*, 21 April 1989). The first session of the congress did not provoke in the USSR the enthusiasm it enjoyed in the West. It was perceived as a total victory of the apparatus, whose interests were unflinchingly defended by Gobachev. But the elections and the Congress had a side effect probably unforeseen by the Party: they contributed to undermine the automisation of Soviet society, without which there is no totalitarian power. Each Soviet citizen discovered he was not alone in his contempt and hatred of communism and that the others thought likewise.

The evolution of the Popular Fronts has been one of increasing radicalisation and progressive loss of Party control. De Tocqueville's celebrated remark springs to mind:

Most often, a people having endured the most grievous laws without murmur, as if without impression, repudiates them violently at any easing of the load . . . the evil suffered patiently as inevitable seems insupportable once the idea of its lessening is conceived.

Besides this evolution fraught with conflict in itself, another destabilising factor is the disparity between the RSFSR, where the Popular Fronts and opposition movements remain marginal and venture fewer demands for democracy, and other areas of the USSR where mass movements are fast becoming politicised. There is also the unremitting economic decline, and the appearance of inflation which may eventually grow to runaway proportions. As Soviet economists point out, 'Incompetent financial policies fertilised the Stalinist system of terror.'[2] Nothing so far indicates that the authorities have decided to adopt a less disastrous financial policy than during the first years of *perestroika*. This, given the circumstances of the USSR, also contains the seeds of violence.

Two factors would seem set to play a decisive role in the coming years: the evolution of Russian nationalism and Party morale. Russian nationalism can only increase. Everything turns on what form it will take. Will the Russians follow Solzhenitsyn, realising that the cure for their own country will follow from emancipation of the Communist empire's subject nations and that the cult of the state and its power threatens to engulf them all? Or will they return to Bolshevism in order to maintain an empire which ruins all its subjects regardless? The same question might occur to the ruling elites. The erosion of ideology may lead them one day to ponder the merits of a power sustained at the cost of wrecking the entire country.

Glasnost has brutally confronted the Soviets with their own underdevelopment, showing them the great gap between them and the civilised nations. This shock treatment could have one of two opposite effects. It may bring about a salutary revival: aspiration to a 'normal' life, with gradual understanding of what that entails – abandonment of ideology and messianism, initiation into democratic modesty (instead of claiming to resolve 'global problems of humanity', the USSR could one day confine itself to working out its own), the desire to understand rather than manipulate, and the taste for freedom. This is the optimist's version. On the other hand, a pessimist would object, not unreasonably, that realisation of Russian backwardness could aggravate the national inferiority complex and cause an explosion of the hatreds cultivated by the regime all these years – hatred of the West, presented by the regime as support for Gorbachev, and hatred of other ethnic and social groups. The world may have yet to discover the implications of the terrible misanthropy bred by communism. Popular explosions, or the threat of them, may provoke a return to the worst sort of tyranny, facilitated by institutions which Gorbachev has created and based on the only two things in the Soviet Union in halfway decent repair: the Army and police.

How can the West cope with this? Its means of influencing the USSR are limited. Gifts of credit and technology are no way to push Moscow along the path of reform.[3] Rather, they give the regime a respite, allowing it to defer changes which are economically indispensable but politically unacceptable to the CPSU. In any case, the state of the Soviet economy is so bad that Western aid can have only marginal effect.

There is a way in which the West can help the peoples of the USSR: by contributing to a rebirth of politics among them. It can give them the example of real freedom in the face of Gorbachevian rhetoric. For that, it will have to throw off the concepts and categories imposed by the Gorbachev propaganda machine, stop meekly reporting that the 'bureaucracy' is the obstacle to reform, that the people must support Gorbachev, and so forth. The West, especially Europe, must reject the 'Apocalypse' blackmail of the Soviet leaders ('the failure of *perestroika* would be a disaster for all mankind', they insist, without noticing that that sort of argument should logically temper the enthusiasm of the Western disarmament lobby). It must stop treating the 'stability' preached by the Kremlin as a value in its own right, and begin to consider possibilities for a post-Communist Europe. One of the objectives of Soviet foreign policy is to implicate and compromise the West in the running of the Communist empire. 'Gorbymania' is of no use to anyone, least of all the peoples of the USSR and Soviet bloc, who already have long experience of Western betrayal. Gorbachev has made the slogan of 'reform' a giant step towards power. The basic contradiction in his position is now apparent. Jean-François Revel's remark that 'the only way to improve socialism is to get rid of it'[4] has been borne out 20 times over by the facts. What will Gorbachev do when it comes to a choice between reform and his own power? Until this moment of truth has occurred, the West's infatuation with him is premature.

One of the main arguments of Soviet propaganda, at home and abroad, is that 'the CPSU is the only political force in the country capable of carrying out reform'. The effrontery of this assertion is made plain by the treatment of those alternative forces (for example, the Karabakh Committee) when they dare to advance political demands. The CPSU takes care to preserve a vacuum which it uses to justify its own power. The West would do well to pay more attention to the expressions of independence in Soviet society, rather than giving the impression of staking everything on Gorbachev. The opposition within the Communist world (and, more theoretically, the West) has to choose between two options: a worn-out totalitarianism ready to make various concessions in order to save its power base, continuing to steer by sight while letting the country sink into economic quicksand, its power weakening in direct proportion to the draining of society exhausted by socialism; or a genuine change of regime.[5] The second choice requires willpower, courage and a great effort. The first is the easy road, but will solve nothing in the end. Sooner or later the day of reckoning will come. We should prepare to face it. The USSR has not yet departed from communism, notwithstanding the obvious signs that the regime is breaking up. The French Revolution did not end with publication of the Register of Grievances. The real crisis is yet to come.

NOTES

1. *Pravda*, 24 February 1989.
2. *Moscow News*, 15 January 1989.
3. The GDR should serve as an example to those who imagine that trade and exchanges will lead to 'convergence' of Communist regimes with democracies. With its economy carried at arm's length by West Germany and the EEC, and constantly exposed to the cultural influences of West Germany, East Germany embodies 'conservatism' in the Communist bloc.
4. See J. F. Revel, 'De la reversibilité du communisme' in *Politique Internationale*, no. 41, 1988.
5. In his most recent book, dealing with the record of 70 years of communism, Zbigniew Brzezinski envisages five possible scenarios for the evolution of the USSR: 'achievement of pluralism', the least probable; lasting crisis, with sporadic explosions mostly on the outskirts; re-Brezhnevisation with a return to centralisation, culminating perhaps in a military *coup d'état* using Russian nationalist slogans; or overthrow of the Communist regime and breakup of the empire. See Z. Brzezinski, *The Grand Failure*, New York, 1989.

Index

Muhri, F., 105
MVD, 50

Nationalism, 34, 57, 68, 74–87, 94, 134
  in armed forces, 116, 121–2
  dangerous element of, 87
  defusing the crises of, 78–83
  ecological problems and, 76–7
  in ethnic minorities and republics, 74, 75,
    77–8
NATO, 98, 99, 100, 103, 107, 108, 124
Natta, Italian communist, 103
Naval Review, 118
Nazarbaiev, N., 52
news media,
  glasnost and, 35, 85
  and military problems, 113–17
Nicaragua, 99–100
Nixon, Richard M., 94
'non-offensive defence', 113, 124
Novosibirsk, 15
nuclear arms, nuclear power, 59, 71, 76,
    101, 102, 103, 107, 108, 123–4, 126–8
  see also anti-nuclear propaganda

Oates, Joyce Carol, 1
oil crisis, 3, 27
Oleinik, Boris, 76
Orthodox Church, 63–70 *passim*, 72, 99

Pamyat 'informal association', 77, 80
Pankraty, Metropolitan, 70
parallel economy, 18–19, 27, 33, 36, 44, 50,
  51
parasitism, 39
Paschezade, Sheikh ul-Islam, 70
Pavlov, 16
perestroika,
  in armed forces, 112–28
  and the church, 69, 72
  and cooperatives, 43–4
  in international relations, 89–109
  introduction of, 16, 17–18, 36, 112
  'new thinking', 92–5
  pioneers of, 21
  problems combatted, 2, 113
  results of, 57–8
  translation of term, 1
  two phases of, 31
    first phase, 36–40
    second phase, 40–60
  Western reaction to and understanding
    of, 4, 55, 58, 97
Peter, the Great, 105
Petrovsky, V., 101
Philaret, Metropolitan, 71
Pimen, Patriarch, 63, 64, 71
Pipes, Richard, 57
Pitirim, Archbishop, 63, 71
Poland, situation in, 46–7, 57, 72, 77, 81,

82, 84, 125
Politburo, 32
pollution, 8–9, 26, 33
Popular Fronts, 53, 79–80, 86, 94, 133, 134
  on Communist Party, 48, 52, 53
  on foreign policy, 91–2, 98, 99, 100, 102,
    104
  on health, 10, 12
  Lenin quoted, 85, 89
  on mafias and corruption, 19–20, 21
  on Orthodox Church, 63–4, 66
  on *perestroika*, 38, 43
  on self-accounting, 83, 84
  on social affairs, 6, 7, 10, 12
  on women, 6, 7
  other references 3, 5, 13, 18, 37, 44, 56,
    81, 105
Primakov, Yevgeny, 86, 91, 94
Prokhanov, Alexander, 86
public health, 33
Public Prosecutor, 53
public transport, 37
purges, 50-1, 52, 79, 118

Quality control commission, 36–7, 38

Rachidov, Sharaf, 17, 18, 19, 20
railways, 12–13
Reagan, Ronald, 68, 96, 112
Reaganism, 3
religion, 63–72, 74, 86
  Lutheran Church, 69
  Orthodox Church, 63–70 *passim*, 72, 99
  unregistered sects, persecution of, 69
Riabtsev, private racketeer, 18
Rust, Matthias, 112, 113, 117
Rybakov, in *Moscow News*, 35
Ryzhkov, on Soviet-Japanese relations, 99

Sakharov, A., 55, 94
scientific socialism, 87
scientific-technological progress, 43, 112
SDI (Strategic Defense Initiative), 108, 112
self-accounting, 41, 42–3, 83, 95, 96
sexual relationships, 4
Shchelokov, Interior minister, 20–1
Shcherbitsky, Ukraine Party Secretary, 85
Shevardnadze, Edouard, 89, 95, 97, 98, 101,
  104
Siberia, 120
Sin, Cardinal, 63
Sinyavsky, 33, 35
smoking, 11
social problems,
  accidents, 12–13, 38, 39
  decapitalisation and poverty,7–8
  ecological problems, 8–9, 59
  the elderly, 15–16, 41
  health, 9–12, 38
  youth, 13–15